ONE AND INDIVISIBLE

ISI.ORG

ONE AND INDIVISIBLE

THE RELATIONSHIP BETWEEN RELIGIOUS AND ECONOMIC FREEDOM

Edited by
KEVIN SCHMIESING

ACTONINSTITUTE

One and Indivisible: The Relationship between Religious and Economic Freedom

© 2016 Acton Institute

Cover image: Pennsylvania State Capitol
Photo credit: David Coleman
Source: iStock

Scripture quotations [unless otherwise noted] are from the New Revised Standard Version Bible: Catholic Edition, copyright © 1989, 1993 the Division of Christian Education of the National Council of the Churches of Christ in the United States of America. Used by permission. All rights reserved.

All rights reserved. No part of this publication may be reproduced, stored in a retrieval system, or transmitted in any form or by any means, including electronic, mechanical, photocopying, recording, or otherwise without the prior permission of the publisher.

ISBN: 978-1-942503-36-1

British Library Cataloging in Publication Information Available

Library of Congress Cataloging-in-Publication Data

ACTONINSTITUTE
98 E. Fulton
Grand Rapids, Michigan 49503
Phone: 616.454.3080
Fax: 616.454.9454

Interior composition by Judy Schafer
Copyediting/Proofreading by Jan M. Ortiz
Cover design by Peter Ho

Printed in the United States of America

Contents

Introduction   *vii*
     Kevin Schmiesing

Part 1
Faith, State, and the Economy: Perspectives from East and West

1. Religious Liberty and Economic Freedom:
   Intellectual and Practical Paradoxes   1
        Samuel Gregg

2. The Contribution of Christianity to the Idea
   of Limited Government   11
        Fr. Martin Rhonheimer

3. Christians and the Challenge of Freedom in the Middle East   23
        Archbishop Maroun Lahham

4. Economic Openness and Religious Repression:
   The Paradox of China   31
        Cardinal Joseph Zen

Part 2
The Relationship between Religious and Economic Liberty in an Age of Expanding Government

5. Preserving Religious Liberty in an Age of Expanding Government   41
        Cardinal Robert Sarah

6. Religious and Economic Liberty and America's Founding   55
        Michael Novak

7. Why Religious Liberty Cannot Prosper without Economic Liberty   69
        Jay W. Richards

Part 3

CHRISTIANITY AND THE FOUNDATIONS OF A FREE SOCIETY: RELIGIOUS, POLITICAL, AND ECONOMIC FREEDOM

8. God, Reason, and Our Civilization Crisis — 85
   SAMUEL GREGG

9. Faith and Freedom and the Escape from Poverty — 95
   ANIELKA MÜNKEL OLSON

Part 4

JUDAISM, CHRISTIANITY, AND THE WEST: BUILDING AND PRESERVING THE INSTITUTIONS OF FREEDOM

10. Zionist Thought on Economic Liberty — 109
    ZEV GOLAN

11. Natural Law in Judaism Revisited — 119
    SANTIAGO LEGARRE

12. Judaism, Natural Law, and Religious Freedom — 131
    DANIEL MARK

13. Private Property, Religious Freedom, and Economic Development — 145
    MICHAEL MATHESON MILLER

Appendix: Remarks on the Concept of Religious Liberty — 159
    MICHAEL NOVAK

About the Authors — 161

Introduction

Kevin Schmiesing

This book is the product of an ambitious three-year program of conferences organized by the Acton Institute. The conferences, conducted in major cities around the globe, brought together scholars of diverse national, religious, and disciplinary backgrounds to discuss the overarching theme of the conference series: What is the relationship between economic freedom and religious freedom?

Several of the essays describe the major events and trends that serve as the backdrop to the conferences and thus to this book. What was an important question in 2012 has only gained urgency in the years between the first conference and the publication of these proceedings.

In the United States, lawsuits filed by Catholic congregations of consecrated religious, by Christian and Catholic universities and businesses, and by other faith-based institutions—some of which have been decided and others of which continue to work their way through the justice system—highlight the increasing tensions between a state determined to regulate the economic and social activities of its citizens and the mediating institutions that have normally provided the social context for individual action. In his first chapter, Samuel Gregg explains how a continually expanding welfare state naturally ends up putting pressure on religious freedom, as government becomes the "paymaster" for religious institutions. Jay Richards later describes the historical and philosophical roots of this developing conflict, underlining how far the United States, in particular, has moved away from a respect for liberty as a corollary of metaphysical conviction regarding the nature of the human person and toward liberty as an expression of philosophical and moral relativism.

In South America, recently dominant populist governments, allegedly focused on the economic empowerment of the poor, have run up against the region's Catholic hierarchy, who have experienced firsthand the ways in which economic and religious freedom are interwoven. Anielka Münkel Olson argues that the poor in Latin America and elsewhere can only be truly empowered by economic freedom—not by state-dominated poverty alleviation schemes—and that religious institutions and ideas have an important role to play in this process.

In the Middle East, Christians face more emergent threats as Islamist groups persecute native Iraqis and Syrians explicitly because of their identity as followers of Christ. Archbishop Maroun Lahham articulates both the positive and the negative aspects of Christians' continued presence in the region that was the birthplace of Christianity. Although Islam is not devoid of its own more liberal tradition on matters of business and state,[1] it is no accident that Muslim advocates of an authoritarian state see government as the arbiter of both religious and economic activity. Here, as elsewhere, the various aspects of freedom tend to hang together.

Building the Framework of Human Freedom

In light of the urgent need both to understand the relationship between religious and economic liberty and to bolster it, it is imperative that the essays here both explore the theoretical basis of the relationship and offer practical guidance for how to nurture it. They must show us how to engage in the building of societies that are at once hospitable to the worship of God and also conducive to the material abundance that permits human flourishing in all its dimensions. They do not disappoint on this score.

Among the significant points of emphases that emerge from these essays is the recognition of a twofold approach to the promotion of economic and religious liberty. Societies that are characterized by freedom in the religious and economic spheres tend both to exhibit strong *cultural* predispositions to liberty and to possess the requisite *institutional* structures that enable and maintain links between religious and economic freedom. Conversely, religiously oppressive and economically stagnant societies normally lack the relevant cultural and institutional forces.

---

[1] See, for example, Mustafa Akyol, *Islam without Extremes: A Muslim Case for Liberty* (New York: W.W. Norton, 2011); and Benedikt Koehler, *Early Islam and the Birth of Capitalism* (Lanham, MD: Lexington Books, 2014).

The Culture of Freedom

In his essay, Michael Matheson Miller cites John Paul II's well-known claim that the "fundamental error of socialism is anthropological in nature," rather than economic.² The pope recognized that socialism, thought by many to be merely an economic system, was in fact more than that. It articulated and enforced certain ways of thinking and acting. In John Paul's words, socialism operated under the illusion that "the good of the individual can be realized without reference to his free choice."³ The kind of human person to which the Russian and Eastern European experiments gave rise has been called *homo sovieticus*: a personality characterized by ennui, lack of trust, and disregard for others' needs.⁴

It is not only in the notorious totalitarian societies of the twentieth century that religious and economic freedoms have been submerged, however. In his first essay, Samuel Gregg reveals one of several paradoxes that must be comprehended to appreciate fully the challenge of preserving genuine liberty. Religious and economic liberties are not ends in themselves or absolutes, Gregg explains: They are rooted in the truth about human persons and they are means to human flourishing. This is why cultures ostensibly obsessed with personal freedom are in fact susceptible to threats to religious and economic freedom. If freedom comes to mean "doing whatever I want," then political and economic spheres will inevitably become battlegrounds where interest groups engage in power struggles so as to gain the upper hand and thereby claim the spoils of victory—financial and otherwise.⁵ In such a climate, genuine religious freedom will be sacrificed on the altar of personal liberation, and genuine economic freedom will be trumped

---

² Pope John Paul II, Encyclical Letter *Centesimus Annus* (1991), no. 13.

³ Pope John Paul II, Encyclical Letter *Centesimus Annus*, no. 13.

⁴ Stephen Bartulica, "The Market Is Not Enough: Moral and Economic Culture in Post-Communist Croatia," in *The Spirit Matters: Reflections on Economics and Society 25 Years after the Fall of Communism*, ed. Kevin Schmiesing (Grand Rapids: Acton Institute, 2014), 56–57.

⁵ The devolution of the concept of freedom has been infamously encapsulated, in the American context, by a line from the US Supreme Court's majority opinion in a case that preserved the supposed right to abortion, *Planned Parenthood v. Casey* (1992). "At the heart of liberty," the justices avowed, "is the right to define one's own concept of existence, of meaning, of the universe, and of the mystery of human life."

by radical egalitarianism and baseless claims to an expanding panoply of economic rights.

That is to say, a real culture of freedom is not the same as a culture of license. At the heart of culture, it must be remembered, is one's answer to the ultimate questions, including the nature of God.[6] There is, then, a mutually reinforcing relationship between cultural norms and politico-economic systems. It is not possible to understand the culture of the West—even the postmodern and post-Christian West—without understanding the inheritance of the Judeo-Christian tradition.

Several essays explore the specifically Jewish dimension of this tradition. Zev Golan recounts the history of Zionist thought on economics and politics. Though the record is mixed, he argues that there is a liberal (freedom-oriented) stream within Jewish nationalism, represented notably by Theodore Herzl and Zev Jabotinsky. Santiago Legarre, drawing heavily on the scholarship of David Novak, summarizes the importance of natural law in Judaism and its similarity to Christian ideas about politics. Legarre's insistence that positive law must be consonant with natural law dovetails with the forceful arguments of Daniel Mark, who exhorts Jews to promote the natural law within the public sphere, for the sake of both Jewish interests and the common good. Specifically, Judaism can improve contemporary culture by refocusing on the obligation side of the concept of rights and by emphasizing the centrality of the "community of believers"—a source of authority outside the purview of the state.

Father Martin Rhonheimer similarly sees in Christianity a corrective to the concept and reality of expansive state power. Notwithstanding superficial views of the history of Christianity as oppressive rather than liberating, the truth of the matter, Rhonheimer insists, is that the theological and political "deep structure" of Western civilization is one that curbs state power by separating religion and politics. There has certainly been mixing and conflation of political and ecclesial authority throughout Christian history, and the result has often been pernicious. But the political absolutism that emerged during the Enlightenment and culminated in twentieth-century totalitarianism was not an outgrowth of Christianity; it was a rebellion against

---

[6] "At the heart of every culture lies the attitude man takes to the greatest mystery: the mystery of God." Pope John Paul II, *Centesimus Annus*, no. 24. Michael Matheson Miller, drawing on the historian Christopher Dawson, makes the same point in his essay in this volume.

the limitations on state power that the Church had always embodied and championed.

Samuel Gregg's second essay provides the link between culture and the institutions of freedom. Gregg argues that the rule of law—an institutional characteristic indispensable to both religious and economic freedom—can only be grounded securely in a sound notion of God and human reason. In this way, the institutional framework necessary for sustaining economic and religious freedom is ultimately dependent on a healthy culture—that is, one that is at least approximately consistent with the truth about God and the human person, the truth that a number of our authors, following centuries of Jewish and Christian tradition, call the *natural law*.

The Institutions of Freedom

If a sound culture is a necessary foundation for freedom, sound institutions are the necessary structure that must be built atop. Jay Richards affirms both the connection between culture and institutions and also the relation between economic and religious freedom by arguing that the "philosophical basis" for promoting economic freedom is the same as that for defending religious freedom: individual rights, freedom of association and family, and limited government. Michael Novak, focusing on the American experience, identifies three institutions vital to economic freedom: private property; freedom of association; and a legal regime of patents and copyrights. Anielka Olson, in her treatment of Latin America, similarly cites private property, rule of law, freedom of exchange, families, and a culture of trust as necessary components of a thriving society.

These overlapping lists point to the centrality of private property and freedom of association as bulwarks of both forms of liberty. (Rule of law may be seen, as noted in Gregg's essay cited above, as the *sine qua non* for the creation and maintenance of the other institutions.)

The institution of private property is at the root of economic freedom. It is hard to conceive true freedom within the economic sphere without the capacity to work and then to possess remuneration for one's labor. Yet the importance of privately owned property extends far beyond its value as a source of individual material wellbeing. Owning property, with the right of disposition that it entails, provides at least a modicum of freedom of action, and this freedom extends to religion. The state-sponsored destruction of churches in China described by Cardinal Joseph Zen could not happen in a place where the property rights of religious individuals and organizations were secure.

The crucial historical role of the Church that Fr. Rhonheimer describes—a source of authority independent of the state—has been to a large extent enabled by its status as the owner of substantial property. That the wealth of the Church has sometimes been a source of temptation, corruption, and scandal is well known and undeniable. But the obverse side of the same coin is that the Church's possession of land, institutions, and other resources represents a real obstacle to those who would seek absolute control over society. It is no coincidence that despots from Henry VIII to Joseph Stalin have made confiscation of Church property a high priority. As the late Fr. Richard John Neuhaus put it, for totalitarians, "Individual religious belief can be dismissed scornfully as superstition, for it finally possesses little threat to the power of the state." Religious *institutions*, however, "that bear and promulgate belief in a transcendent reality by which the state can be called to judgment ... threaten the totalitarian proposition that everything is to be within the state, nothing is to be outside the state."[7]

In addition to its role in preserving religious liberty, Michael Matheson Miller observes, property ownership enables economic development, changes the outlook of those who gain title—by increasing feelings of trust and a sense of responsibility—places limits on the state, and promotes healthy family life. Again, we come up against one of the paradoxes that characterize the discussion of religious and economic liberty: Individual ownership of property that is properly circumscribed within a rule of law, though sometimes thought to give rise to a radical individualism, in fact enables and promotes vibrant communities and social institutions.

Promoting Freedom Today

Promoting freedom, then, means promoting the culture and institutions without which it cannot thrive. It also means recognizing the ties that bind freedoms to each other: When one falls, there is risk that it will pull the others down with it. Like so many of our authors, Daniel Mark sees a close connection between religious liberty and its cousins: "In building and preserving the institutions of freedom in our time, we would do well to promote the centrality of religious freedom not only for its own sake but

---

[7] Richard John Neuhaus, *The Naked Public Square: Religion and Democracy in America* (Grand Rapids: Eerdmans, 1984), 82.

also because it undergirds all of our rights." Similarly, for Michael Novak, religious liberty is "deeper and more basic" than economic liberty but the two are nonetheless closely connected, for economic liberty permits human persons to "multiply, survive, prosper, and have the wherewithal to practice their religious faith publicly."

Although the dominant theme of this book is the strong correlation between economic liberty and religious liberty, the essayists well understand that the connection is not a direct and simple one. That the two dimensions of human freedom tend to move in tandem does not mean that they always and everywhere march in lockstep. Cardinal Zen points out the tension between the two that can be observed in China where increasing latitude for individual initiative in the economic sphere has been accompanied by continuing government oppression in the religious sphere.

One dimension of the fight to preserve economic and religious freedom, therefore, must be an insistence on a limited scope of action for government. Cardinal Robert Sarah pithily summarizes the point, and at the same time brings us full circle—back to the intrinsic link between liberty and anthropology. "The danger is this," Cardinal Sarah writes: "When God is taken out and religion gets crowded into a corner by government expansion with citizens forced to put aside their religious convictions, society not only excludes the great contribution of religion but also promotes a culture that redefines man as less than what he is."

Encouraging the human person never to be "less than what he is" is a worthy cause. It applies universally to the rich and poor, the "global North" and "global South," to Jew, Christian, Muslim, and atheist. All stand in need of a deeper understanding of the truth and the resolution to conform their lives to it. This was the point made by Pope Benedict XVI in his provocative Regensburg Address, which is cited in the essays by Samuel Gregg and Archbishop Lahham. That Benedict's characteristically careful, sensible words should be provocative is itself a measure of the state of public discourse in the twenty-first century.

What did Benedict say? He insisted that reasonable discourse was the only legitimate way for the world's peoples to engage each other. Radical pluralism of viewpoint—Christian, Muslim, agnostic—would naturally give rise to violent encounter if the parties did not instead commit themselves to peaceful encounter. Benedict warned against the idea that unreasonable action (e.g., killing in the name of religion) might in fact be consonant with the nature of God. He did not claim that irrational theology is uniquely Islamic; such errors can be found in Christian thought as well. And he argued that religion (of the reasonable type), rather than fostering superstition and fantasy, actually promotes genuine engagement and understanding of reality. Thus, dogmatic secularism wrongly excludes theology and metaphysics from intellectual life, shriveling human reason by restricting it to the empirical and material.[8]

To this clarion call for peaceful and reasonable dialogue, many around the world—whether accurately informed of the pope's remarks or not—responded with irrational outbursts and, in some places, physical violence. The position of the pope, and by extension the Church, as defender of the capacity of human reason and the dignity of the human person, was thereby made clearer—at least for those with eyes to see. The situation has been confirmed by Benedict's successor. "Today more than ever," Pope Francis wrote in his first encyclical, "we need to be reminded of [the] bond between faith and truth, given the crisis of truth in our age."[9]

Our common humanity obliges us to pursue the truth and to live according to its tenets concerning the nature of reality. Economic and religious freedom are the fruits of this understanding and commitment, and are in turn the means to enable every human being to be fully the person he was created to be. May this volume make at least a modest contribution toward that end.

---

[8] Pope Benedict XVI, "Faith, Reason, and the University: Memories and Reflections," Lecture of the Holy Father, University of Regensburg, 12 September 2006. http://w2.vatican.va/content/benedict-xvi/en/speeches/2006/september/documents/hf_ben-xvi_spe_20060912_university-regensburg.html.

[9] Pope Francis, Encyclical Letter *Lumen Fidei* (2013), no. 25.

Part I

FAITH, STATE, AND THE ECONOMY: PERSPECTIVES FROM EAST AND WEST

1

Religious Liberty and Economic Freedom

Intellectual and Practical Paradoxes

Samuel Gregg

My subject is religious liberty and economic freedom. Concerning the first of these freedoms, one hardly need say that religious liberty is a subject of some urgency for many Christians today. In fact, in some cases, it is now literally a matter of life and death. Every day, it seems, we read of the brutal killing of Catholics and other Christians in the Middle East, in Africa, and in some parts of Asia. Sometimes this has more to do with ethnic and political rivalries than religion *per se*. It is also true that at least some of the violence against Christians flows precisely from antagonism toward Christianity as a religion.

Certainly in Western Europe and North America, the situation is different. Yet it is hard to deny that some governments and particular shades of political opinion seem eager to empty the very concept of religious liberty of any meaningful content. Often this is done, strangely enough, in the name of tolerance. Such measures also reflect a longer history of antagonism toward two specific aspects of Christianity on the part of what might be called secular progressivism. The first antagonism is toward the orthodox Christian vision of morality. The second antagonism is toward the Christian claim that some forms of social organization are not subject to endless manipulation by the state: most notably, marriage, family, and the Church itself.

Although it is the religious liberty of Christians that is most regularly violated today, the Catholic argument for religious liberty does not simply concern the well-being of Christians. After all, if a government can nullify or suppress religious liberty, it is surely capable of repressing any other civil or political freedom. To that extent, non-Christians, agnostics, and atheists also have a stake in maintaining strong protections for religious freedom. But curiously enough, it is rare—in fact, extremely rare—for defenders of religious liberty to list economic freedom as one of the rights that can be easily suppressed once religious liberty is effectively undermined.

Thus, I would like to take time to discuss some important aspects of the relationship between religious freedom and economic liberty. As has been mentioned, the relationship is complicated and not always straightforward. Therefore, I will limit myself to three points. First, I want to illustrate how unjust restrictions on economic liberty often flow from efforts to restrict religious freedom. Second, I consider how expansionist welfare states can result in subtle but significant corrosions of the liberty of the Church. Third, and more positively, I suggest that, in some situations, a growth in economic freedom could create pressures for enhanced religious liberty.

The Connection between Economic and Religious Freedom

Today most people are accustomed to thinking about religious liberty as a prerequisite for political freedom. This is perhaps because one of the most prominent unjust restrictions on religious liberty has been formal limitations on the ability of members of particular faiths to participate fully in public life. A good example is that of Catholics who lived in the England of Elizabeth I and James I in the sixteenth and early seventeenth centuries. During this period, the English parliament passed a series of acts that gradually stripped Catholics in England of most of their political rights because of their refusal to conform to the Church of England.

The limitations on the freedom of Catholics, however, went beyond this. Usually overlooked, but perhaps even more damaging, was the state's usurpation of the property and economic freedom more generally of English Catholics. This came in the form of crippling fines levied on recalcitrant Catholics by governments that, not coincidentally, were short on revenue. Successive governments also placed restrictions on the type of commercially related activities that Catholics were allowed to pursue. It was even made difficult for Catholics to bequeath their property to Catholic relatives. Incidentally, similar economic restrictions were endured by those Protestants who refused to conform to the Church of England, many of whom consequently chose to migrate to America.

I suspect that many people, including many Americans, do not know that many of these infringements on the freedom of Catholics crossed the Atlantic. Note, for instance, the colony of Maryland. Named after Charles I's Catholic queen, Maryland was founded in 1632 by English Catholics fleeing religious repression. Interestingly, these Catholics insisted on religious tolerance for *all* Christians in their colony. This resulted in the 1649 Maryland Toleration Act: perhaps the first law ever passed that guaranteed religious liberty to every Christian confession.

Unfortunately, anti-Catholic laws similar to those in England eventually prevailed in Maryland. For our purposes, however, we should note that economic motives played just as significant a role as anti-Catholic animus in driving this change. As the most famous of Maryland Catholics, Charles Carroll of Carrollton—the only Catholic to sign the Declaration of Independence and the wealthiest man in the American colonies at the time—observed, "Selfish men invented the religious tests to exclude from posts of profit & trust their weaker or more conscientious fellow subjects."

Here is one of the paradoxes of suppressions of religious liberty. Limiting a religious group's participation in political life often results in members of that group focusing on economic success. Consider, for instance, the case of those perennial entrepreneurs: Arab Christians.

Until the beginning of the twentieth century, Christians, overwhelmingly Catholic and Eastern Orthodox, constituted almost 25 percent of the Middle East's population. Less well known is the fact that Middle Eastern Christians traded extensively with their co-religionists throughout the Mediterranean for centuries. They thus played a major role in facilitating East-West commercial exchange between the Christian and Muslim worlds. Here it is worth noting the increasing evidence assembled by contemporary scholars such as Rodney Stark, which suggests that most of the early Christians did not, in fact, come from the impoverished segments of the Roman Empire's population.[1] Many early Christians, it turns out, were well-educated aristocrats, most notably women. However, an even larger number were Hellenized Jews and what were called "God-fearers," living and working in commercial ports around the Mediterranean. Early Christianity, it appears, was a mostly middle-class religion.

---

[1] Rodney Stark, *The Rise of Christianity: A Sociologist Reconsiders History* (Princeton, NJ: Princeton University Press, 1996).

Obviously, the particular economic success of Middle Eastern Christians has something to do with geography. Another cause of their commercial success may well have been the second-class legal status imposed on most Arab Christians from the seventh century onward. In his monumental *History of the Arab Peoples*, the Oxford Arabist and historian, the late Albert Hourani, relates that Christians in most of the Middle East were forced to wear special clothes identifying them as non-Muslims.[2] They were also obliged to pay a special tax, frequently banned from carrying weapons, and inhibited from broad participation in political life. Hourani notes, however, that these constraints resulted in many Christians' focusing their energies on those aspects of the economy where they were allowed some liberty. Eventually, Middle East Christians dominated, according to Hourani, many spheres of economic life throughout the region, including merchant shipping and banking.

A similar tale can be told about the Jewish people. In the not-so-recent past, being Jewish meant that you could not participate in politics or serve in the military or civil service in the Christian and Muslim worlds. Many Jews were consequently left with little else to do but create wealth in those areas of the economy where they were permitted to flourish.[3]

Now, I hasten to add that these stories of economic success are *not* a good reason to suppress the religious liberty of any group. Indeed, a subsequent problem is that economically successful religious minorities often become the target of governments. Sometimes this results from governments' seeking to increase their revenue. On other occasions, it occurs when governments look for a convenient group to blame for their own political and economic failures.

THE SECULARIZING WELFARE STATE

Let me move, however, to my second observation: the ways in which more gradual, more subtle infringements of economic freedom can undermine religious liberty. Here, I want to specifically reference the welfare state. Since the time of the modern welfare state's founding by Otto von Bismarck, it has steadily expanded in most Western countries. Today the government,

---

[2] Albert Hourani, *A History of the Arab Peoples* (1991; repr., Cambridge, MA: Harvard University Press, 2010).

[3] See Thomas Sowell, *Migrations and Cultures* (New York: Basic Books, 1997).

according to the Organization for Economic Cooperation and Development, consumes a minimum of 40 percent of annual gross domestic product in virtually all Western European nations. The vast majority of this spending is on welfare programs.

The modern welfare state is of course predicated on the willingness of governments to significantly limit economic freedom. You cannot have large welfare states without more regulation, more taxes, and some redistribution of wealth. All such choices corrode, to some extent, economic freedom. To varying degrees, all Western governments, including the United States, have judged that it is worth having less economic freedom and slower wealth-creation in return for the economic security that some believe is realized through welfare states.

Now many people, including myself, have been critical of this choice. In the first place, the economic sustainability of the modern welfare and regulatory state is questionable, especially given the below-replacement birthrates prevailing in almost all European nations. Nor is it clear that welfare states have in fact provided economic security. If you doubt this, then just ask the millions of young Europeans today who cannot find employment. Then there are the ways in which welfare states have contributed to the development of some very unhealthy political dynamics—and not just in Europe but also much of America.

What has this to do with religious liberty? Put simply, there is considerable evidence that welfare states and the inevitable associated reduction of economic freedom have negatively impacted the Church's institutional liberty. Throughout much of the West, many Catholic charitable institutions collaborate very closely with state welfare agencies. In some cases, they are heavily funded by the state. Furthermore, in most instances, these Church organizations are subject to all the same regulations as those of state welfare institutions, albeit with some exemptions concerning activities that the Church regards as intrinsically immoral.

Part of the problem is one of philosophy and culture rather than economics *per se*. Today, as the distinguished American Catholic historian James Hitchcock observes, welfare states are thoroughly grounded on secularist assumptions about human beings.[4] To the extent that the secularist vision of life reflects a hedonistic and nominalist view of man, it is obviously quite

---

[4] James Hitchcock, "The Welfare Snare," *Touchstone*, May/June 2012, http://www.touchstonemag.com/archives/article.php?id=25-03-003-e.

different from the vision of the person found in classical Christian anthropology and the natural law. Clashes between these visions explain some governments' efforts to force Catholic welfare agencies to align themselves with particular secular government welfare practices.

The other dimension of the problem is surely the nature of the modern welfare state itself. It tends to encourage monolithic approaches to social and economic issues. That is partly because of the welfare state's top-down approach to social problems. It is also partly a result of its inevitably bureaucratic character.

This situation has created two problems for the Church. The first is that, to the degree that church organizations directly work with, or in some cases, have become virtually subsumed into the welfare state, their independence of action becomes compromised. The second is that there is considerable evidence that government-funding of church-outreach programs to those in need tends to make such institutions susceptible to secularist ways of thinking. As the funds from state contracts begin constituting a significant part of Catholic organizations' financial resources, their culture can easily change. Reliance on such support creates incentives for church organizations to avoid confrontations with state authorities about how they do what they do and why they do it. It is not unknown, for instance, for Catholic organizations receiving or seeking government contracts to subtly downplay their Catholic identity. They thus slowly cease to be institutions that partake of the *Libertas Ecclesiae*. Instead, they start morphing into what George Weigel aptly describes as "mere vehicles for the delivery of state-defined and state-approved 'benefits,'"[5] rather than seeking to live out Christ's commandment to love our neighbor in ways consistent with the truth revealed by Christ to his Church.

Then there is the depressing fact that acceptance of state funding can encourage many people working in Catholic organizations to begin viewing the state as their primary master. Again, this should not be surprising. If 70 percent of a Catholic charity's income is derived from government subsidies and contracts, the government *has* effectively become their paymaster.

Of course, the Church has nothing in principle against Catholic organizations working with governments for purposes such as outreach to the poor. Nor does it regard being a recipient of public funding as intrinsically

---

[5] George Weigel, "All In for the First Amendment," *NationalReview.com*, September 10, 2012, https://www.nationalreview.com/nrd/articles/314763/all-first-amendment.

problematic. Given the ways in which accepting such funding can subtly diminish the liberty of the Church itself, however, now is surely the time for Catholics to ask ourselves some hard questions about the general prudence of continuing to accept government financial assistance.

Increasing Economic Freedom Leads to Religious Liberty

There is, however, another way to think about this issue. This involves considering the third question on which I want to briefly reflect: how growth in economic freedom might affect religious liberty. In this regard, Mainland China is a good example of how *expansions* of economic freedom can create pressures for enhanced religious liberty in authoritarian societies.

Since the early 1980s, China has embraced some economic freedom. Of course, China is also plagued with corruption, and what is often called crony capitalism pervades much of the Chinese economy. The Chinese Communist Party, military, and government remain major shareholders in hundreds of Chinese businesses, including, most worryingly, its banking system. All these factors, I suspect, will cause China some significant economic problems in the not-too-distant future. That said, China is unquestionably more economically free and open to the global economy than it was during the dark years of Chairman Mao.

Less well known, however, is that it is precisely in those Chinese provinces that have been permitted to somewhat liberalize their economies that millions of Chinese have embraced Christianity. This should not surprise us. Why? Because once you grant more liberty in one area, it is hard to stop freedom from spreading to other spheres of life. Economic liberty, for instance, requires and encourages people to think and choose freely. Without this, entrepreneurship and free exchange are impossible. It is, however, difficult to limit this reflection and choosing to economic questions. People start asking social questions, political questions, and, yes, religious questions. In addition, many Chinese—in fact, millions of them—have decided that Christianity is *the* answer to their religious ponderings.

This has created immense dilemmas for China's rulers. On the one hand, the regime claims to value many religions' contribution to public life. China's president, for instance, has indicated that China is "losing its moral compass" and that religion can "help fill a void that has allowed corruption to flourish."[6]

The Chinese regime also knows that Christianity in particular denies that the state can exercise any religious authority over the church. Such a claim is unacceptable to China's present rulers because it implicitly challenges the ruling elite's monopoly of power. Hence, we should not be surprised that the regime persecutes Catholics who insist on loyalty to the pope. And not just Catholics! In one of China's wealthiest eastern provinces, Zhejiang, evangelical churches are being told to remove their crosses and are threatened with having their buildings demolished. Why? Because "too many Chinese" are embracing Christianity. Even more surprising, however, is that evangelical preachers are *publically* denouncing the government's actions.

Now, as social scientists rightly remind us, correlation does not mean causation. The fact, however, that many evangelical preachers in this economically successful and increasingly Christian Chinese province are publically telling the authorities to back off does tell us something. It tells us that once the freedom genie is out of the bottle, it is very hard to put it back in. Plainly, religious freedom is not yet a reality in Mainland China. As figures such as Cardinal Zen will attest, the treatment of many Christians, especially Catholics, by the regime remains deplorable. But, I would suggest, thanks partly to China's somewhat haphazard market-liberalization, pressures for a fuller realization of religious liberty seem to be growing within China.

Conclusion

The three examples of the relationship between religious liberty and economic freedom that I have explored all too briefly illustrate the ways in which different forms of freedom can reinforce each other, but also how corrosions of liberty in one area can damage its vitality in other spheres. One remaining issue, however, is how the Church can better reflect upon these realities.

Answering that question requires a longer discussion but a good start would be for the Church to give as much attention to the conditions that favor true economic freedom in the twenty-first century as the Church gave throughout the twentieth century to the conditions that promote authentic

---

[6] Benjamin Kang Lim and Ben Blanchard, "Xi Jinping Hopes Traditional Faiths Can Fill Moral Void in China: Sources," Reuters, September 29, 2013, http://www.reuters.com/article/2013/09/29/us-china-politics-vacuum-idUSBRE98S0GS20130929.

religious liberty. The role of economic liberty in contributing to human flourishing and the common good remains, I would respectfully suggest, insufficiently appreciated in modern Catholic social teaching. This may be because of the Church's traditional and necessary attention to distribution issues. It may also owe something to the fact that much of the frame of reference for modern Catholic social teaching remains locked in the context of nineteenth-century Western European industrial capitalism: an economic world that no longer exists.

When, during the Second Vatican Council, the Council Fathers considered the subject of religious liberty, they made it clear that their argument for religious freedom was not about tolerance for the sake of tolerance. Nor was it about diversity. It was not even about equality. *Dignitatis Humanae* never said error and truth enjoy the same value. It never said that all religions and all philosophies are equal. In fact, *Dignitatis Humanae* explicitly rejects that claim. Careful readers of the document soon recognize that the Church affirms the religious liberty of individuals and communities as a *precondition* for the honest search for religious *truth*. Truth, Vatican II teaches, is the *foundation* of religious liberty. Vatican II also teaches that truth is the *goal* of religious liberty.

An analogous type of argument needs to be developed in Catholic circles for economic freedom. To be sure, there are plenty of resources in the Church's teaching for developing such a principled case beyond its somewhat fragmented present status. These range from the church fathers and scholastic thinkers to more contemporary writers such as Blessed Antonio Rosmini and Michael Novak. On a broader level, however, the Church's understanding of economic liberty, like its teaching on religious freedom, has a potentially powerful role to play in helping Catholics raise their eyes to the transcendental horizon to which Christ and his Church direct us.

How so? Put simply, the material and economic goods produced through human freedom and enterprise certainly have their own value. But as Pope Francis—and every other pope before him has said—they do not last. Like all worldly things, they eventually disappear from our lives when we are called to meet our Maker to be judged. Those that do last are the basic moral and spiritual goods developed through human choice and action that anticipate the kingdom that is to come. As the Council Fathers proclaimed in *Gaudium et Spes*:

> after we have obeyed the Lord, and ... nurtured on earth the values of human dignity [*humanae dignitatis*], brotherhood [*communionis fraternae*] and freedom [*libertatis*], and indeed all the good fruits of our nature

and enterprise, we will find them again, but freed of stain ... and transfigured, when Christ hands over to the Father: "a kingdom eternal and universal, a kingdom of truth and life, of holiness and grace, of justice, love and peace."⁷

Economic liberty is not, of course, an absolute. Nor is religious freedom. But both *are* rooted in the truth about man that we find in Christian anthropology and the natural law: the truth knowable through Revelation and right reason. In the end, these are the only foundations that make all authentic forms of freedom—religious, political, or economic—to be truly reasonable, to be truly life-giving, and to be truly indivisible. A more radical and a more Catholic message to today's world is, I would submit, difficult to imagine.

---

⁷ Pastoral Constitution on the Church in the Modern World (*Gaudium et Spes*), no. 39, http://www.vatican.va/archive/hist_councils/ii_vatican_council/documents/vat-ii_cons_19651207_gaudium-et-spes_en.html.

2

THE CONTRIBUTION OF CHRISTIANITY TO THE IDEA OF LIMITED GOVERNMENT

Fr. Martin Rhonheimer

In this essay, I would like to share some thoughts on Christianity, markets, and limited government. First, I shall point out why limited government is an indispensable precondition for the development and flourishing of a free-market economy. Second, I will show that Christianity was a necessary condition for limited government in the sense of classical liberal constitutionalism becoming possible both theologically and historically speaking. Finally, I plan to explore why many Catholics have forgotten or do not understand this genuine link connecting limited government, a free-market economy, and Christianity.

LIMITED GOVERNMENT AS A PRECONDITION FOR THE DEVELOPMENT AND FLOURISHING OF FREE MARKETS

Limited government means that state authority and the range of government responsibilities are confined to a limited number of tasks. These tasks consist mainly of guaranteeing the rule of law, that is, a legal order that assures the fundamental rights and liberties of citizens (especially their lives, physical integrity, and property), as well as maintaining internal security and defense against outside enemies. A limited government may also provide public infrastructures and services that cannot be supplied by civil society. Limited government presupposes a clear distinction between the state and society and their corresponding tasks.

Limited government is only possible in a state that is both *minimal* and *strong*. It must be *minimal* in the sense that it does not take on functions that can be fulfilled by civil society itself; nor does it attribute to itself paternalistically the task of being the source of benefits and welfare. The minimal state is, thus, a state that is impeded by constitutional law from expanding beyond certain limits and thereby becoming a menace to citizens' freedom. Such a state, therefore, takes subsidiarity seriously because it considers it illegitimate to assume responsibilities reserved for individuals, the family, civil associations, private entrepreneurial initiative, and all the different kinds of charities.

At the same time, such a state is *strong* in the sense that it imposes the law in an impartial way and without serving, or being usurped by, particular interest groups or constituencies. A minimal and simultaneously strong state provides the framework for a market society by imposing the same rules on everyone and thereby making the market work in favor of the *common good*. Therefore, it leaves civil society with the liberty and the capacity of developing all sorts of profit or nonprofit entrepreneurial and charitable initiatives to meet the special needs of particular groups and individuals. Government should support these initiatives not by subsidizing them (which it can do only with money previously taken from the citizens, hampering thereby citizens' economic capacities) but rather by creating the legal and technical conditions that facilitate them and therewith encouraging citizens to freely engage in such activities. This does not exclude that there exists, preferably on a communal or local level, a public, state-driven safety net in order to make sure that there is no single person unsupported in case of extreme and otherwise insurmountable helplessness.

Now, for such a minimal strong state and, consequently, limited government to be possible, there exists at least one *necessary* condition, or one set of necessary conditions. Without it, limited government cannot possibly become a reality. This condition is that state power does not attribute to itself a religious and redemption-promising function—not even in the sense of being the source of all social benefits and welfare—but that it leaves religion and its institutional representation and authority free as a *counterpart to state power*, thereby impeding state power from becoming all-encompassing and confining it to qualified worldly or specifically "temporal" tasks. This again implies that state power does not understand itself as being the source of moral standards or the ultimate moral criterion for justice and law. Thus, for the very idea of limited government to be able to arise, there has to exist a kind of separation or dualism of (1) politics and religion, as well as of (2) positive law and ultimate moral criteria.

It is only the nonsacral, nonreligious, and not ultimate-truth-claiming and redemption-promising state that is able to accept the limitations proper to limited government.

Now—and this is my second thesis—as a historical matter of fact, it was Christianity and the civilization shaped by it that provided these conditions that not only paved the way but also continuously nourished the soil for a political culture of limited government to come about. With this came the rule of law and fundamental human and civil rights and liberties, and in turn the political framework for a free economy and modern capitalism with its unique wealth-generating potential.

By a great many people in the past and today, however, the Church is seen throughout history as having been a force of oppression, obscurantism, superstition, and opposition to scientific progress. In this view, the Church eventually became the fiercest critic of modern liberties, such as religious freedom or freedom of speech, of the press, and of other civil and political rights. Such a view of history, however, is superficial. It ignores what we might call the theological and religious-political "deep structure" of the history of Western civilization, which we can grasp when comparing the development of Western civilization with the civilization shaped by Islam.[1]

CHRISTIANITY AS A NECESSARY CONDITION FOR LIMITED GOVERNMENT

Notice first that Christianity introduced an absolute novelty into history of which we—the heirs of a culture impregnated with the Christian spirit—are at times not enough aware: the separation of religion and politics and, conversely, the independence of political power—and even more so the independence of the legal order—from being defined on the basis of religion

---

[1] See Martin Rhonheimer, *Christentum und säkularer Staat. Geschichte - Gegenwart - Zukunft* (Herder: Freiburg i. Br., 2012); and an earlier version of this book can be found in Rhonheimer, "Christianity and Secularity: Past and Present of a Complex Relationship," in *The Common Good of Constitutional Democracy: Essays in Political Philosophy and on Catholic Social Doctrine* (Washington, DC: Catholic University of America Press, 2013), 342–428; see also Larry Siedentop, *Inventing the Individual: The Origins of Western Liberalism* (Cambridge, MA: Harvard University Press, 2014) also in Penguin Books, 2015.

and its sacred texts (which precisely is the condition I mentioned above). According to the nineteenth-century French scholar Fustel de Coulanges, "Christianity was the first religion that did not want to make the law depend on religion."[2] We can say more generally: for the first time in history, Christianity recognized that temporal things—politics and the juridical institutions of the earthly city—respond to an intrinsic logic that is legitimately autonomous and independent from revealed religion because it roots in the logic of creation and of being as distinguished from the logic of salvation.

Precisely in this, Christianity is distinct from all other ancient civilizations, even if in Greek philosophy and in Roman law prior to the Principate the tendency to such autonomy already existed. This explains why Greek philosophy and science and Roman law could easily become part of a civilization shaped by Christianity. It is also why they were so fruitfully transformed by Christianity and handed on to posterity.[3] In this, Christianity is radically distinguished from Islam, which arose later and introduced exactly the opposite principle. Islam, in fact, defines politics and the law on the basis of revealed religion and its sacred texts, claiming that religion, law, and politics have a single source, thus discrediting any other natural source of truth. In Islam, there is no distinction between the order of creation and the order of salvation. As a consequence, in a Muslim context, government cannot have principled limits whatsoever, and most importantly *it cannot be limited by religion itself.* On the contrary, in an Islamic understanding, politics must be *submitted* to and be *part of* the logic of revealed religion.

It is not an exaggeration to say that the Christian duality of politics and religion, as well as of creation and salvation, is the central theme and the leitmotif of Western history—though not in the sense that religion and politics, the sphere of church and state, were always unmixed, let alone separated from each other. There were many reasons, some legitimate, some illegitimate, for continuous intersections but also subsequent clashes between church and state power. Precisely these permanent and regularly returning

---

[2] Numa Denis Fustel de Coulanges, *La cité antique* V, 3 (1864 ; repr., Paris: Flammarion, 1984), 463.

[3] Cf. Vittorio Mathieu, *Il fondamento romano e cristiano della laicità, in L'identità, in conflitto dell'Europa. Cristianesimo, laicità, laicismo,* ed. Laura Paoletti (Bologna: Il Mulino, 2005), 157–69.

clashes have become typical for the development of Christian civilization. The following are some highlights relevant in the present context.[4]

The first stand taken by church leaders, especially by some popes and bishops in union with them (in particular Saint Ambrose of Milan and Saint Athanasius), regarding the relationship between church and state power was provoked by the battles for the church's freedom against the caesaro-papist interference of the emperors. They had adopted Arianism, which led emperors to understand themselves as bishops of the church, continuously interfering in religious affairs. To preserve the "secular" concept of the temporal power was the real impact of the anti-Arian struggle that lasted more than a century.

At the same time, the Catholic fight against the Arians and thus against caesaro-papism in the first centuries of Christianity does not change the fact that even then the Church considered it correct that the Catholic religion be raised, as religious truth, to the rank of the official religion of the state. To understand this post-Constantinian evolution one should bear in mind that during these first centuries the Catholic bishops, and Christians generally, were Romans and acted with a Roman mentality. This mentality, rooted in the imperial tradition, continued to include the idea of political-religious unity, and especially the idea of the need to venerate the true God for the health and prosperity of the earthly city. When the shock of Alaric's invasion of Rome happened in 410, this was not only a political blow, but also, and perhaps above all, a religious one, causing the remaining pagans to rejoice and the foundations of the imperial Roman theology, by this time based on Christianity, to shake.

Against the danger of the triumph and revival of paganism, Saint Augustine reacted with his epochal work *De civitate Dei*, in which he takes a crucial step: he dissolves, again, the perilous link between empire and church, between political prosperity and religious truth. At the theoretical level, *De civitate Dei* signified the abandonment of Roman imperial logic. Saint Augustine's political thought could have served as a new point of departure for a clear separation between religion and politics, and in this sense could have contributed to the emergence of a merely secular and limited understanding of the temporal power without any claims of a religious dimension.

This did not come about because of many contingent factors. The breakdown of the Roman Empire converted Church administration and the

---

[4] For more details and references, see my *Christentum und säkularer Staat*, cited above.

bishops into the guardians of public order, including public administration. The popes allied with the Frankish kings, and, finally, under Charlemagne restored the Roman Empire of the West. So-called political Augustinianism, a one-sided and—in my view—incorrect interpretation of Saint Augustine triumphed. According to political Augustinianism, it was the task of the temporal power of kings and emperors to serve the supernatural end of the Church. This eventually led to a sacralization of temporal power and its growing self-understanding as having a religious and even ecclesiastical function, supporting with the coercive means of temporal power what the spiritual authority of the bishops and priests could not achieve by their word and predication alone. In turn, however, the Church became increasingly integrated into the political system of the Empire—bishops being elevated to the rank of temporal princes.

It was Pope Gregory VII who reacted against this system. It was a harsh reaction, a real "papal revolution," as it is called by legal historians.[5] This papal revolution aimed to reestablish the dualism of politics and religion, and to simultaneously proclaim the superiority of the spiritual over the temporal power not only as a matter of principle, but also in terms of legal superiority and of the *plenitudo potestatis* of the pope.

We have to understand what the substance of this papal revolution was, because it was not, at least regarding its—perhaps unintentional—consequences, of a restorative or reactionary kind but just the opposite. By revitalizing the separation of religion and politics, claiming the superiority of the spiritual over the temporal power, it actually paved the way to modernity. To understand this, we have to grasp the crucial importance of this typically Christian dualism of politics and religion that was reestablished in the eleventh century: the inherently Christian resistance on the part of the Church (especially the pope) against what I call the "totalization of the political."

According to Church tradition, fully reestablished in the High Middle Ages through the "papal revolution" initiated by Gregory VII, the Church maintained that the temporal rulers of this world—emperors, kings, and other princes—are also subject to moral standards that are ultimately interpreted by the spiritual authority of the Church. These popes thus claimed that earthly rulers, being *faithful* sons (and daughters) of the Church, are subject in moral matters to the judgment of the spiritual power.

---

[5] See especially the landmark study by Harold J. Berman, *Law and Revolution: The Formation of the Western Legal Tradition* (Cambridge, MA: Harvard University Press, 1983), 85.

This in fact was based on a long tradition. One is reminded of the famous formula created by Pope Gelasius at the end of the fifth century: "There are two powers governing this earth: the sacred authority (*auctoritas sacrata*) of the popes and the royal power (*potestas regalis*)."[6] This formula is in fact in continuity with the other, earlier, formulation of St. Ambrose of Milan: *Imperator intra ecclesiam, non supra ecclesiam* ("the emperor is in the Church, not above the Church").[7] Gelasius declared that the emperor is not a bishop of the Church, but a son of the Church. The Church, therefore, claims to assess—always on the basis of pastoral criteria—the exercise of temporal power, and this judgment is essentially a judgment on the actions of the *person* who represents this power. It is clear that this subordination remains within a strictly pastoral logic and makes use of exclusively spiritual means.

Yet, by claiming the *plenitudo potestatis* and by elaborating a full system of church law and jurisdiction with a central papal curia, the papacy of the High Middle Ages, starting with Gregory VII, did indeed assume a political role. Admittedly, it did so for pastoral reasons. But by jurisdictionally interfering in the order of temporal power by means of canon law and the logic of feudalism—by deposing princes, kings, and excommunicating emperors—its pastoral interventions inevitably became political. This is why the papal *plenitudo potestatis* started to be challenged by the logic of the rising modern territorial state and its claims of sovereignty and juridical autonomy. This was the origin of modern absolute—that is, institutionally uncontrolled—political power—an absolutism that was favored by the religious scission after the Reformation and the creation of the confessional state in order to establish religious peace (but not religious freedom). *It was this system of the confessional, absolute state* (to which the Catholic Church had allied itself)—and not the medieval system of papal *plenitudo potestatis*—that later was challenged by classical liberal constitutionalism. The political doctrine of liberal constitutionalism proclaimed, against absolute and arbitrary state power, the rule of law, government control by parliamentary representation, and an independent judiciary that guaranteed the submission of political power to the law.

---

[6] Hugo Rahner, *Kirche und Staat im frühen Christentum* (Munich: Kösel-Verlag, 1961), 256. (The English translation is my own.)

[7] St. Ambrose of Milan, Speech against Auxentius (Migne, Patrologia Latina 16, 1007–1018), cited by Hugo Rahner, *Kirche und Staat im frühen Christentum* (Document 13b), 184.

My point is that such ideas could not have been developed in a civilization shaped by the idea that law and politics have to realize an order established by sacred texts and interpreted by religious authorities. Instead, they spring from the much different heritage that the Church had left to posterity. Therefore, precisely in the very moment when the papacy reestablished the genuine Christian dualism of spiritual and temporal power, it set free the dynamics of what was the essence of this culture of Christian dualism: the idea of morality and law being independent from and antecedent and superior to the political power of any earthly government, and that, therefore, there exist liberties and rights, as well as standards of good and evil—natural law—to which government must submit and that other legal and political institutions must guarantee.

In fact, the doctrine of the great popes of this period reduced temporal princes, including the emperor himself, to common laymen. They radically *desacralized* the temporal power, thus creating the conditions for the formation of a new secular spirit in civil and political life. The merit of the papal revolution was the relativization of political power and the creation of a public juridical culture. This is why the eleventh century is considered by most historians nowadays as the real beginning of an evolution that led to the rise of the modern state and, in turn, to its "taming" by the classical liberal idea of state power being subject to the rule of law, civil liberties, and the corresponding constitutional restraints—the essence of limited government.

It was not contingent to this logic that the papacy, during the battle against the messianic claims of Emperor Frederick II in the thirteenth century, promoted and protected the independence and liberties of the Italian city-states, empowering them to create what was the first example of a capitalistic economy with a banking and trading system spreading from Florence to Flanders, England, and as far as Ireland. It was for the most part Spanish absolutism invading the Italian peninsula (except Venice), which by its autocratic methods and hampering of economic liberty stopped this dynamic. In fact, as Rodney Stark has shown, there is a clear link between economic backwardness and absolutism.[8] Where freedom was given by the rulers, as in England and in the Netherlands, trade and economic innovation could flourish. There, it was first Catholic Antwerp that developed high levels of economic creativity and where capitalism succeeded. This economic culture

---

[8] Rodney Stark, *The Victory of Reason: How Christianity Led to Freedom, Capitalism, and Western Success* (New York: Random House, 2006).

was destroyed by Spanish absolutism. By imposing absolutist rule, it made entrepreneurs, merchants, and bankers, with their experience and skills, move to Amsterdam, which as a part of the Netherlands turned to Calvinism and subsequently became independent from Spanish rule. The Dutch did not embrace Calvinism for religious reasons but to become independent from Spanish absolutism and to maintain their traditional liberties inherited from the Middle Ages. This is one of the sad and influential chapters of Catholic anticapitalism, which for Spain turned out to be economically pernicious.[9]

THE FORGOTTEN LINK AMONG LIMITED GOVERNMENT, A FREE ECONOMY, AND CHRISTIANITY

There are comprehensible historical reasons for the Church's alliance with modern absolutism. Those reasons also existed during the nineteenth century for the Church's opposition to the classical liberal claims for a free society and civil liberties; mainly religious freedom, freedom of the press, freedom of association, and, to some extent, to freedom of trade. This opposition is a paradoxical fact, given that these classical liberal claims are a typical offspring of a civilization shaped by Christianity. The clash between liberalism and the Church in the nineteenth century is certainly due to the totalitarian, antireligious, and anti-Church aspects of the French Revolution and subsequent liberal and republican anticlericalism in traditionally Catholic countries. It was also the consequence of grave misunderstandings on the part of Church authorities concerning the nature of the liberal idea of limited government in general, of civil liberties in particular, and of a free-market economy in an age of industrialization and capitalism.

One very influential example of such a misunderstanding was Bishop Ketteler of Mainz, a key pioneer of modern Catholic social doctrine. Like many Church leaders in the nineteenth century, Bishop Ketteler considered freedom of trade, industrialization, and capitalism as a way to permanent misery and oppression of laborers. By 1860, Bishop Ketteler was convinced of the accuracy of the Socialist Ferdinand Lassalle's "iron law of wages," according to which workers would never be paid wages above the level of

---

[9] See Stark, *The Victory of Reason*, 161.

subsistence. This, said Lassalle, is why the state should determine wages according to workers' needs.[10]

As we know today, Lassalle, and with him Bishop Ketteler, proved to be absolutely wrong. However, Ketteler's and similar kinds of criticism of capitalism and industrialization created a Catholic tradition built on myths of a "wild" and cruel capitalism; of a free market that was unjust and in need of state intervention into the mechanism of prices and wages to become civilized; and of the need to bring about social justice by correcting market outcomes by redistribution.

Many Catholics today do not only think in such patterns, but they are even convinced that these policies are required by sound moral standards and Christian social doctrine. Their often uninformed views about economic matters leads them to think that large-scale redistribution can be realized without, in the long run, gravely damaging the common good and the interests of the less well off and the poor. This long-term damage becomes more and more evident these days.

However, it is surprising that, despite his errors of judgment concerning the wealth-creating potential of industrialization and capitalism, Bishop Ketteler and other Catholic leaders who engaged in resolving the so-called social question actually did not at all advocate what today's social-minded Catholics seem to see as a requirement of the gospel. In his famous book *The Question of Workers and Christianity* (1863), Ketteler clearly opposed "a System of taxes and coercion which ruins nearly all states and in which free self-determination and love of freedom become absolutely irrelevant."[11] He added: "We notice how the idea of a system of taxation and coercion becomes more and more prevalent and how, in this way, the modern way manifests that it is alien to all principles of true liberty. Christianity leads individuality to its full freedom; the modern spirit destroys individuality even in regard to property."[12] Similarly the Catholic priest Christian Hermann Vosen—a close friend of Blessed Adolph Kolping, the founder of the *Gesellenvereine* ("Journeymen's Unions")—advocated, according to the

---

[10] Wilhelm Emmanuel Freiherr von Ketteler, "Die Arbeiterfrage und das Christenthum" ["The Question of Workers and Christianity"] in *Sämtliche Werke und Briefe*, by Wilhelm Emmanuel Freiherr von Ketteler, ed. V. Erwin Iserloh (Mainz: v. Hase & Koehler Verlag, 1977), Abteilung I, Band 1, 377.

[11] von Ketteler, "Die Arbeiterfrage und das Christenthum," 417.

[12] von Ketteler, "Die Arbeiterfrage und das Christenthum," 417.

principle of subsidiarity, support of their associations of self-help by the state but was clearly opposed to any kind of organized help to workers by the state itself. He argues, "State help is guardianship and will end for single persons in slavery, even if the state is a republic."[13]

Now, the people who thought this way were pioneers of modern Catholic social doctrine. The reason they did not understand the real merits of capitalism, despite clearly foreseeing the despotic and financially ruinous character of what would later develop to be the "social state" and the "welfare state," was a lack of understanding the intrinsic tendency of a capitalistic economy to enrich everybody by progressively increasing workers' productivity and real wages and therewith the prosperity of *all*. However, what survived in most of Catholic social thinking was not these thinkers' clear defense of freedom and self-responsibility but their mostly uninformed and widely disproved accusations of the alleged dangers and failures of capitalism. These errors have since that time led to the pernicious spiral of state interventions, followed by corresponding distortions of market processes, which again legitimate the call for correcting and regulating state intervention, thereby creating new disequilibrium and distortions.

I am convinced that if these pioneers of modern social Catholic thinking lived today and knew that their gloomy predictions concerning the deprivation of laborers through capitalism had proved wrong, they would consider state intervention to redistribute income and property through high taxes with the aim of establishing so-called social justice (understood as some kind of economic equality) to be illegitimate. They would also consider illegitimate a state system of social security that, in the sense of the welfare state, renders citizens dependent on state services and the state bureaucracy, thereby destroying self-responsibility and the social nets of solidarity, especially the family.

In fact, all such interventions of government into the economy and into society by which the state to a large extent assumes the functions of what individuals, families, and civil society could and should do, is an insidious violation of the principle of subsidiarity. It is both morally corrosive and economically inefficient and, as we all know, has eventually led to increasing public debts, which, if not confronted, will ruin state finances, cause inflation,

---

[13] Christian Hermann Vosen, "Zwischen Lassalle und Schulze-Delitzsch: Staatliche Hilfe zur Selbsthilfe," in *Katholizismus und Sozialismus in Deutschland im 19. und 20. Jahrhundert*, ed. by Wolfgang Ockenfels (1864; repr., Paderborn: Schöningh, 1992), 42.

and thereby enrich the wealthiest at the expense of the economically most disadvantaged.

This is why I think it is time for Catholics to overcome the myths of the past and to rediscover truly limited government as a condition both of liberty and of a society in which personal responsibility and solidarity—mainly the solidarity net created by the family but also by the free association of citizens—are not continuously undermined but instead stimulated and encouraged. This is also why I think it is time to understand that Catholics should not be advocates of a social justice that makes citizens more and more dependent on state welfare, but that, precisely as Christians, they first should be defenders of freedom and with that defend personal responsibility and free entrepreneurial initiative to meet the real needs of their fellow citizens, especially the poorest and most needy among them. It is not states or governments that are the source of wealth and general prosperity but the creativity and inventiveness of entrepreneurs and generally of citizens' entrepreneurial activity of the most diverse kinds, including in the nonprofit and charity sectors. These can flourish only in a free-market economy that, in turn, presupposes limited government that refrains from legislating social justice in this way, an activity that is bound to gravely damage the common good.

3

CHRISTIANS AND THE CHALLENGE OF FREEDOM IN THE MIDDLE EAST

Archbishop Maroun Lahham

I would start by saying that it is difficult to speak similarly about all the churches of the Arab world. These different institutions obviously have much in common, but each also has specific traits. I am going to try to be as comprehensive as possible. In my description, I am going to present three parts: (1) an overview of the churches in Arab countries, (2) the common positive achievements of these churches, and (3) the difficult issues facing these communities.

OVERVIEW

The Arab countries that I am speaking of are Egypt, Jordan, Palestine, Syria, Lebanon, and Iraq.[1] Christians from the Middle East have been Arab and Christian since the first centuries. That is to say, they are not Muslim Arabs converted to Christianity. It may be useful to remember that Christianity was born in Palestine. Between the second and seventh centuries, Middle Eastern countries were 80 percent Christian. This percentage went down only slowly: 50 percent at the time of the crusades, 20 percent in the nineteenth century.

---

[1] I am including neither the countries of North Africa outside of Egypt nor the countries of the Persian Gulf because Christianity vanished centuries ago in those places, and because the current churches of the Maghreb countries almost all include expatriates from dozens of countries, mostly African.

Right now (in 2014), outside of Lebanon where Christians represent one third of the population, the percentages of Christians range from 10 percent in Egypt to 6 percent in Syria (before the civil war beginning in 2011) to 4 percent in Iraq, 3 percent in Jordan, 2.5 percent in Israel and 1.2 percent in Palestine. You will notice that the percentage of Christians goes hand in hand with political and social instability. The churches of the Middle East have been called "the churches of Calvary." They gladly embrace this calling, but they also know that after Calvary comes the resurrection.

Before investigating the numbers, we must be aware of two facts: First, several Arab governments do not provide an official number of Christians because of both political and social considerations. Second, numbers in the Orient are rounded out and are often subjective. Hence, we consider that the number of Arab Christians ranges between 15 and 20 million, half of whom are in Egypt. Christians belong to four church families: the Catholic Church, the Orthodox Church, the Oriental Orthodox Church (which predates the Council of Chalcedon) and the Protestant churches. Each family in turn is home to multiple communities, such as different rites or denominations. I cannot explore this diversity in detail here; however, I note that the question of the rite in the East is so important that Arab Christians define themselves by their liturgical rites more than by their ecclesial denomination. In the Middle East, we are Latin, Maronite, Copt, Syriac, Armenian, or Chaldean before being Catholic or Orthodox.

Concerning Jordan, it is part of the Holy Land not only as a church (it belongs to the Patriarchate of Jerusalem) but also because several holy places of the Old and New Testaments are located in Jordan. These include the site of Christ's baptism, Mount Nebo (from which Moses viewed the Holy Land), and the site of the martyrdom of Saint John the Baptist. In Jordan, Christians number between 220,000 and 225,000, or 3 percent of the population, spread in a mosaic of churches. The three most important are the Greek Orthodox Church, the Latin-Rite Catholic Church, and the Eastern-Rite Catholic Church, each with its own clergy, parishes, and educative and social works. The absolute number of Christians in Jordan is constantly rising, but proportionally their numbers are decreasing. This is not just due to emigration, which exists but has not reached hemorrhagic levels as in Palestine, Iraq, or Syria, but mostly it has to do with a declining birthrate. (When Jordan was created in the 1920s there were about 25,000 Christians, a number that rose to 150,000 in the 1960s and to between 200,000 and 250,000 today.) The origins of Jordan's Christians lie in two sources. Some are of Jordanian descent while the others are Palestinians who arrived in 1948 and in 1967. It is worth noting that Christians from the Eastern bank of the Jordan are not less numerous than those who came from Palestine and that marriage between the two peoples is slowly erasing the distinction.

Before considering what was achieved and what is still under discussion, I point out an aspect that is specific to Jordanian society and possibly also to the Iraqi one, both Muslim and Christian: tribal speech and practices. In the two countries, the family, small or extended (the tribe) is the custodian of values, the guarantor of social and political order. At the political level, for instance, the landscape is not drawn according to parties but rather according to tribal loyalties. Some Christians, especially those of Jordanian origin, are just as susceptible as Muslims to the allure of tribal identification because they share the same social structures as the Muslims, and to a large extent they also share the same social values—patriarchal values where solidarity among individuals and families is built according to kinship.

Positive Achievements among Middle East Christians

The first achievement is that Arab Christians are fully integrated in society throughout most of the Middle East. They are Arabs and this fact is accepted and assumed, although on different levels. I make this point because some Christians in some Arabic countries tend to trace their affiliations back to distant historical lineage (Phoenician in Lebanon, Pharaonic in Egypt, or Chaldean in Iraq). However, the countries that constitute greater Syria (Syria, Jordan, and Palestine) are the most Arabized countries. They have never thought of themselves as being anything other than Arab.

Second, aside from Egypt (and until recent civil strife),[2] Arab Christians have enjoyed a peaceful and favorable situation for the past few decades regarding their presence in their respective lands, a situation that was guaranteed by regimes that were attached to their stability. They are quite obviously an essential component of the Arab society. Some Western writers and journalists dare to say that Arab Christians are protected by their political regimes, to whom they have vouched an unwavering loyalty. Indeed, we have seen some manifestations of this during the Arab Spring in some

---

[2] Editor's note: Regarding references to "recent" events throughout this essay, note that Archbishop Lahham's remarks were delivered in April of 2014.

countries, especially in Egypt and Syria. While this is true, it is so only up to a certain point. In fact, we should not consider the Arab Christian communities like a herd that blindly follows the regime to protect itself against the vast Muslim majority that threatens to crush them. On the contrary, they are also concerned by the nascent political divisions of the Arab world, and Christians may find themselves either at the highest levels of government or in the opposition.

Third, this favorable situation means that Christians have been members of successive governments, as well as of parliaments. For a very long time, almost all Arab governments have included at least one, and sometimes two, Christian ministers. It is even more obvious in Jordan. Out of the fifty senate seats, whose members are directly nominated by the king, there are six Christians, or more than 10 percent, and almost three times their demographic numbers. Out of the 150 Parliament seats, ten belong to Christians, which is three times their demographic representation. As for the public sector, they are notably present in the economy (35 percent of the country's economy is controlled by Christians, ten times their demographic numbers.) They can also be found in the diplomatic sector, the financial sector, and even within the military command—with the caveat that some very high administrative or military functions have remained difficult to access. (There is some justification for this. For instance, the highest-ranking military officers have to lead prayers on some occasions.) This Christian presence in social and economic life is common to all Arab countries. It is even more obvious in Lebanon.

Fourth, Arab Christians enjoy total freedom of worship (except in Egypt), including the building of churches and other religious buildings. This freedom works well within ecclesiastical courts, which are the only ones competent to deal with questions of marriage and inheritance according to a personal status. In Jordan, the Council of Heads of Churches—created by order of the king and also by the king's cousin, Prince Ghazi, who is responsible for relations with the Christian communities—is the lawful partner to deal with religious questions at an official level. For instance, it is this council that allows (or blocks) government recognition of a new church settling in Jordan. Arab churches, especially the Catholic ones, are recognized for their contributions to education and health care. Some Arab countries with socialist tendencies (Syria, Egypt, and Iraq) had nationalized Christian schools in the 1960s, and they recently reversed their decisions. The educational and healthcare institutions they run provide churches with an important social visibility, which allows them to step out of the boundaries of religious practice. They create an internal cohesion within these communities and forge a specific identity. They also allow them to transfer their values to the thousands of Muslims who attend their schools, not to mention the contacts with all the students' parents who are not always Christians.

To conclude this positive look at the presence of Arab Christians in the Middle East and about the dialogue of life with their Muslims compatriots, I quote a paragraph from the famous letter of October 2007, from 138 Muslim theologians to then-Pope Benedict XVI and to the Christian religious leaders following the pope's famous Regensburg Lecture. It reads:

> Muslims and Christians together make up well over half of the world's population. Without peace and justice between these two religious communities, there can be no meaningful peace in the world. The future of the world depends on peace between Muslims and Christians. The basis for this peace and understanding already exists.[3]

DIFFICULT ISSUES FACING MIDDLE EAST CHRISTIANS

All is not well in life and that is especially true for Christians in Arab countries. They are faced with difficult situations, which have created unease in their daily lives. These issues vary somewhat from one country to the next.

The status of a minority. Arab Christians are well aware of their minority status. They accept it, however reluctantly. The uneasiness stems from their centuries-old position as minorities, which has forged a fragile psychological state. It has translated into a quest for outside protection, cultural isolationism, exaggeration of innocuous facts, the fear of coming out in the public square, and so on. We also should mention the other side of this coin, the psychology of the majority, which limits the rights of minorities, always following the law of the strongest. In the East, we would rather speak of "small numbers" than of "minority"; we would rather say that the presence of Christians is not just about percentages but also about a quality of presence, and that rights and duties are rooted in the dignity of the human person with no concern for numbers.

Mixed marriages (Muslim/Christian). Marriages between people of different church affiliations are a widespread and universally accepted fact, but

---

[3] "A Common Word between Us and You," October 13, 2007, www.ACommonWord.com.

Muslim-Christian marriages are rare because of the patriarchal character of Arab society, both Christian and Muslim. When it happens, especially when a Christian young woman marries a Muslim young man, the woman is rejected by her family. The interfaith life is a daily occurrence in Arab countries (for studies, work, and social relations) but this all stops when it comes to marriage. What strengthens this refusal on the part of the families and the churches is the fact that mixed marriages can only go one way as far as Islam is concerned. A young Muslim man can marry a Christian woman but a Christian youth cannot wed a Muslim woman, unless he agrees to convert to Islam. For this reason, churches in Arab countries do not usually bless mixed marriages, even if Canon Law allows it. There is no easy solution; any other arrangement goes against the Muslim Sharia law. We need Arab civil societies, with a clear separation between the mosque and the state. The Arab Spring proved that it is not impossible, but it takes time.

The school curriculum. With one or two exceptions, the school curriculums of Arab countries speak very little to the Christian past of the countries before the arrival of Islam. Yet, these places were 80 percent and more Christian up until the seventh century. Dozens of Arab bishops attended the councils of Nicea, Constantinople, and Chalcedon—on the agreements of the last there was even the signature of a bishop for the nomadic Bedouins (the "bishop of the tents"). In teaching and in history books, mosques and other places of worship are mentioned, but not the word *church*, which never comes up in Jordanian books.

Religious teaching. In all Arab countries, with the exception of Jordan, religious teaching, Muslim and Christian, is a mandatory class. Christian schools in Jordan provide religious teaching to Christian and Muslim students—to each their "catechism." However, public schools only offer Muslim religious teaching, and the Christian students receive no religious schooling. In 1997, a law was almost passed to introduce catechism for Christian students in public schools, but the arrival of the Muslim Brotherhood at the Jordan Department of Education in 1998 all but blocked its implementation.

Freedom of conscience. In all Arab countries, except for Lebanon, Tunisia, and Algeria, religious freedom means freedom of worship. Freedom of conscience, in the true sense, which is to freely choose your faith, does not exist and proselytism is completely banned. There are countries where conversion to Christianity is punished by death (Morocco and Iraq). In other countries, the law clearly forbids the conversions, but the social pressure is usually enough, more so than the law, to convince people to stay with their religious communities of origin. This works both ways, although Christians converting to Islam will not encounter any serious danger, while the other way around is more complicated and risky (normally stopping short of the death sentence called for by Sharia in cases of apostasy).

The rise of Islam. Since the 1970s, and more specifically since the Iranian revolution, Arab countries are witnessing a rise in Islamic fundamentalism. New forces coming out of Muslim civil society are confronting the various powers that be and requesting that life and public spaces be made more Islamic. We are seeing various aspects of this in a growing Islamic public discourse, educational content, TV programs, a multiplication of construction of mosques, and the obligation to publicly respect the Ramadan fast. All of this is challenging the previous balance, although only partly. Thus, in many ways today, Arab Christians are made to feel like a dwindling demographic and social minority. They are feeling invaded and threatened by the religious, social, and political demonstrations of Islam. This general unease was reinforced by the Islamist dominance of some Arab regimes recently elected. However, we have to notice that faced with the failures of Islamist regimes in Egypt, Tunisia, and Libya, not to mention the Islamist threat in Syria, the Islamist movements are lowering their profiles. The future remains difficult to predict.

CONCLUSION

The future of Arab Christians hangs in the balance. Before the events of the Arab Spring, they were enjoying a favorable and relatively stable situation. For this demographic minority, the moderate political powers were a major guarantee of protection, which allowed them to obtain a proportionally larger political representation and recognition that was the source of religious, social, and economic development. For the past three years (2011–2014), the Arab world has been jolted in ways that nobody was expecting and that have irresistibly changed society. Everyone was affected, including Christians. Again, we must wait to see what the Middle East will look like once the dust settles. No matter what happens, it is up to the Arab Christians to take up the challenge of their presence and not to rely exclusively on political circumstances, whether favorable or not. To this end, they will have to work on promoting religious dialogue, on being open to others who are different, on conviviality, and on their unwavering commitment to the Arab land.

4

ECONOMIC OPENNESS AND RELIGIOUS REPRESSION

The Paradox of China

Cardinal Joseph Zen

Economic openness and *religious repression*—these two facts are before our eyes, and they seem to be in contradiction. I invite you to follow me in glancing at the first fact from my post of observation and to look a little deeper into the second fact; then I will put a question mark on the word paradox.

ECONOMIC OPENNESS

There is an almost universal admiration and gratitude for the powerful leadership of Mr. Deng Xiaoping, who dared to open the Chinese economy, freeing it from the dogmatic constraints of a rigid Marxist socialism. Private property became legitimate and private enterprise was encouraged. Getting rich is now honorable, and economic reform is the solid truth. Foreign investments were invited, China became the world's factory, and cheap products invaded the world market.

There is a saying that "Beijing people love their country, Fukien people leave their country, and Shanghai people sell their country." (That is, they sell the land to foreign developers.) But that seems to be no longer a peculiarity of Shanghai. Everywhere, governments take the land from the people—with poor compensation—and sell it to generous buyers.

Chinese tourists can be seen everywhere (including in Saint Peter's Square, where one often hears Mandarin being spoken), and they have an astonishing spending capacity (not to mention those who arrive at Hong

Kong shops and Macao casinos with suitcases filled with cash). They buy properties in every city of the world to the point of destabilizing property markets.

Many people admire the wisdom of Mr. Deng Xiaoping for saying "no matter whether a cat is black or white, the important thing is that it can catch mice." But this is a nice way of affirming a very nasty tenet of Stalinism: anything goes that can strengthen the Party—that is the only norm of truth. After the disaster of the Cultural Revolution, the Chinese Communist Party needed to turn to capitalism to save itself.

In a few years' time, China has become a world economic power: the Chinese miracle. But it is no miracle, with totalitarian control of the country and a huge army of cheap labor. National production rocketed in a short time. But who benefited from it?

Surely a big portion has gone to the national treasury, and many people could emerge above the poverty line, but Deng Xiaoping also said: "Let a few get rich first." Who are those few? Power and money are inseparable, and power is in the hands of the Party.

From time to time, cases of corruption are revealed, and they always involve sums measuring in the billions. This should be no surprise, considering what can happen when, in a totalitarian system, you have an economic reform without a political reform. Such scandals are bound to happen.

There is an international group of journalists who are investigating the riches of Chinese leaders and their families. The chief editor of a prestigious newspaper in Hong Kong has given his name to the group. He was ambushed recently by a professional assassin and was seriously—almost fatally—wounded.

Religious Repression

There is no denying that with the economic openness the scenario of religious repression is very different from the past.

In the past, religion was officially declared to be the opium of the people. At the beginning of the People's Republic, foreign religious leaders were arrested, accused, publicly tried, and expelled—some clamorously like the papal nuncio Monsignor Riberi; some after years of imprisonment like Bishop Walsh.[1]

Then the local clergy were forced to accept complete control of the Church by the government. Those who refused were put in prison or sent to labor camps where they stayed for twenty, or sometimes thirty, years. Among these are my Salesian confreres: seminarians, priests, and brothers, more than a dozen of them. For many years, we lost contact with them. They belonged to the silent Church. Half of them died in prison. The survivors surfaced toward the end of the 1970s to tell us the moving stories of their witness to the faith.

When the Cultural Revolution was launched in the 1960s, even those who had accepted the control of the government went to prison or labor camps. Churches were turned into factories, go-downs (warehouses), or simply closed. Religion disappeared from the surface of society.

Today, visitors to China can see the flourishing of religious life. Many churches have been restored, and new ones have been built. People can pray and sing and receive the sacraments. Catholic seminaries have been opened. I had the privilege of teaching in the seminaries of Shanghai, Xian, Wuhan, Shijiazhuang, Beijing, and Shenyang from 1989 to 1996. All the seminaries were crowded with seminarians, between one hundred and two hundred of them. We, teachers from abroad, were granted full freedom to teach (though my lessons were recorded in Shanghai at the beginning).

Like other citizens, priests and other consecrated religious can go abroad rather easily. Many priests, seminarians, and nuns can pursue their religious studies in Catholic institutions in Europe, the Americas, and the Philippines. Buddhists could even hold huge international conventions with people from the Religious Bureau acting as assistants for organization and security matters.

Is not all this marvelous? Yes, but everything is still completely under the control of the government.

When the open policy started at the beginning of the 1980s, those who went to prison at the beginning of the fifties were freed from prison. By that point they had no reason to change their position. They went underground.

Actually there are so many different situations. In cities such as Shanghai, the underground Church is literally underground. Priests celebrate mass in

---

[1] Cardinal Antonio Riberi (1897–1967), a native of Monaco, was nuncio to China at the time of the Communist Revolution. He was expelled shortly thereafter, in 1951. Bishop James Edward Walsh, MM (1891–1981), was an American missionary who arrived in China in 1918. He was arrested in 1958 and released in 1970.

private homes, obviously tolerated by the government. In the countryside, government officials constantly keep an eye on them. They are outlaws, so they are constantly harassed and can be arrested.

Other priests, who were put in prison during the Cultural Revolution in spite of their previous obedience to the government, now have been assigned back to the churches that are being reopened one after another. Years of suffering and isolation made them reflect, and they now desired to be reunited with the Universal Church. Many old bishops, ordained illegitimately, asked the Holy Father to legitimize them. Young bishop candidates, elected according to the government-imposed method, asked the Holy Father to approve their ordination. In many cases, after due investigation, legitimizations and approvals were granted by the Holy Father, wisely advised by Cardinal Tomko, then Prefect of the Congregation for the Evangelization of Peoples.[2] Cardinal Tomko comes from Czechoslovakia, knows the communists well, and managed the things of the Church in China with great wisdom. He upheld clear principles but was also open-minded and understanding toward the real situation.

All this could not escape the attention of the Beijing government. Such a show of loyalty toward Rome pushed them to put on a show of force. In January 2000, they planned an illegitimate ordination of twelve bishops in one ceremony. It failed. Only five candidates showed up, and the seminarians of Beijing seminary boycotted the ceremony in which they were supposed to serve. In September, the government staged a big campaign against the canonization of the Martyr Saints of China.[3] All the Chinese bishops were called to Beijing to sign a letter of protest against the pope, accusing some of those martyr-missionaries of being imperialists and having committed horrendous crimes against Chinese people. This campaign was not a complete success either, even if several bishops surrendered.

At the end of 2000 came the retirement of Cardinal Tomko as Prefect of the Congregation for the Evangelization of Peoples. Unfortunately, his successor was not up to the difficult job and five years passed with a com-

---

[2] Cardinal Jozef Tomko, born in what is now Slovakia, was Prefect of the Congregation for the Evangelization of Peoples (formerly the Congregation for the Propagation of the Faith) from 1985 to 2001.

[3] The Martyr Saints of China were 120 Catholics who were killed between 1648 and 1930. They were canonized by Pope St. John Paul II on October 1, 2000.

plete void of thinking and action—or, rather, he acted by inertia, and the Chinese Communists took advantage of it and strengthened their position.

Cardinal Ratzinger was elected pope in 2005. He was knowledgeable about the situation of the Church in China. In 2000, as Prefect of the Congregation for the Doctrine of the Faith, he took part in the last of those special *combined* and *expanded* meetings for the Church in China.[4]

Pope Benedict XVI appointed an Indian cardinal with a long career in Vatican diplomacy as the next Prefect of the Congregation for the Evangelization of Peoples. The pope's intention was probably to honor the Asian Churches. Unfortunately, the new cardinal prefect's long diplomatic career under Cardinal Casaroli made him a convinced devotee of Ostpolitik.[5]

Pope Benedict could not do more than what he did for the Church in China. He wrote a wonderful "Letter to the Church in the People's Republic of China" in 2007 and shortly afterward he set up a huge special Commission for the Church in China (with all the officials of the Secretariat of State and of the Congregation for Evangelization of Peoples, plus some experts from the Vatican, such as the Prefect of the Congregation for the Doctrine of the Faith and experts in Canon Law, completed with five bishops and a dozen experts from Hong Kong, Taiwan, and Macau—in all some thirty persons).

During its first three years, the commission met four times a year: one plenary meeting lasting three full days and three standing committee meetings lasting a half-day each. In the following years, the standing committee met only once a year for a full day.

Alas, it is really beyond understanding that all this commission's work could be spoiled and wasted by some people who were stubbornly convinced of the miraculous efficacy of Ostpolitik. They manipulated the Chinese translation of the papal letter. They defended an obviously distorted interpretation of an important statement of the letter. They ignored some points of clear consensus of the commission.

Once I asked the retired Anglican Archbishop: "what would you say about your friend our Pope Benedict?" "He is very shy," he answered. For long years, our shy Pope Benedict tolerated the cardinal whose action was

---

[4] *Combined* refers to the fact that the meetings consisted of personnel from both the Vatican Secretariat of State and the Congregation for Evangelization of Peoples. *Expanded* means that there was participation from bishops and experts from the frontline of Hong Kong and Taiwan.

[5] Italian Cardinal Agostino Casaroli (1914–1998) was Secretary of State for the Holy See from 1979 to 1990.

obviously at variance with his direction. In order not to irritate the Chinese Government, Cardinal Dias[6] did not appreciate the courage of the courageous in their resistance to the government but did encourage the weak ones in their submissiveness.

At one time, the government used mainly the method of threat to induce people to obedience. Government people threatened punishment of the disobedient and their relatives. They could come to you and say, "It seems that your brother has some problem at his work place, do you want us to put a good word in for him?" If you say, "Yes, please," you become a slave. If you say, "No, thank you," they go to his work place and tell his superiors to fire your brother.

Your mother may be sick. They come to you and say, "Do you want us to send a car and bring your mother to the hospital?" If you say, "Yes, please," you are their slave. If you say, "No, thank you," they go to the hospital and tell them not to accept that old lady.

Now, the Chinese Communists are rich; they can employ the even more efficacious weapon of allurement, that is, the offer of big sums of money and of honorable positions in society like membership in the People's Congress or in the Political Consultative Body at different levels.

Some Catholics reluctantly collaborate with the government; some, whom Pope Benedict characterizes as opportunists, do so all too willingly. In the meantime, the underground community feels it is unappreciated, considered inconvenient; it feels almost abandoned. (When the old underground bishops die, they are not given successors.)

Before his retirement, Pope Benedict XVI intervened strongly to stop that wrong policy, but the Church in China had already been brought to a miserable situation. The Chinese government has succeeded in enslaving the leadership of the official community and keeps harassing the underground community.

The religious oppression, more than in physical suffering, consists in humiliation. There is a lay Catholic, Mr. Liu Bainian, who nominally was the secretary of the Patriotic Association but who in reality is the supreme authority of the official Church (he is probably a Party member). Now he has retired and has been named the Honorary President of the Patriotic Association, but we know that he is still working full-time.

---

[6] Cardinal Ivan Dias, formerly Archbishop of Bombay, was Prefect of the Congregation for the Evangelization of Peoples from 2006 to 2011.

When, in 1993, I started teaching in the seminaries in Beijing, they offered me a banquet. Mr. Liu was at the head of the table. There were five or six bishops at the table, but nobody said a word; only Mr. Liu kept the conversation going. Whenever he left the table, everybody was eager to speak.

I was teaching in the National Seminary when I discovered that the rector, Bishop Zong Huai De, who was also the President of the Patriotic Association and the Chairman of the so-called Bishops' Conference (the highest authority of the official church), could not make an international call from his office but had to go to the apartment of Mr. Liu across the road.

The government can dispose of the bishops as if they were objects. To force the legitimate bishops to take part in illegitimate episcopal ordinations, they go and take them, put them in the car or on the train or the airplane without telling them the destination. Once arrived at the destination, they are put into hotels, their room well guarded. The next day they put the liturgical vestments on them and bring them up to the altar.

Cardinal John Tong wanted to visit Canton, where he grew up, together with the Bishop of Essen (Germany). The government wanted them to see all four bishops of the province (among them there is one who is excommunicated). Cardinal Tong objected to this plan. The government then took the Bishop of Canton away, so that Cardinal Tong and the bishop from Essen could not meet any bishop.

They force our people to act against their consciences. They do not want to make martyrs but renegades. Unfortunately, they succeed in a good measure—in part also because of the loss of direction on our side, fruit of a misguided policy in the Roman Curia. The Church in China could be like the Church in Poland, but now is more like the Church in Hungary in those years of Ostpolitik.

I would like to hope that Pope Francis may operate the same miracle as Pope John Paul II did with Cardinal Tomasek of Czechoslovakia. From a fearful downhearted victim of the communists, John Paul II turned him into a courageous fighter for religious freedom. (I highly recommend the reading of *The End and the Beginning* by George Weigel,[7] especially the first chapter "the End ... that is the victory of freedom.")

---

[7] George Weigel, *The End and the Beginning: John Paul II—The Victory of Freedom, the Last Years, the Legacy* (New York: Random House, 2011).

Paradox or Contradiction?

Is there any contradiction between economic openness and religious repression? No—if you look at them only from the position of the interest of the Party. The Communist Party is supreme; anything to defend the Party is good and legitimate.

Now both economic openness and religious oppression are necessary for the survival of the Party. Has the economic openness caused much corruption in the Party? They say: "Let us fight the corruption." But they cannot understand that corruption comes from power, and absolute power causes absolute corruption.

Is there a strong demand for religious freedom? It cannot be granted, they say: The Party must be able to control the conscience of the citizen. So they grant a fake freedom. Their whole system is built on lies.

One pastoral letter of Bishop Jin Luxian of Shanghai bore the title, "Witness to Truth." In that letter he said that one of the four Chinese characters that appear most frequently nowadays is the one meaning "fake." You have fake food, fake medicine, poisonous milk, buildings that collapse at the first tremor of an earthquake. And superiors do not like to hear the truth.

There is *no* true Bishops' Conference in China. The Patriotic Association is just an instrument in the hands of the government to control the Church. Nowadays the Party is "running" the Church; they do not even try to save appearances.

"The Bishops' Conference revoked the approval of Bishop Ma's ordination," they said. But you can see the photo of the Conference: Mr. Wang Zuoan, the Director of the Religious Affairs Bureau, sits smiling at the center of the presiding table with Bishop Ma Yinglin and Bishop Fang Xingyao at his sides with heads bowed down.

I am an old man; I cannot wait too long to see the victory of freedom in China. So I recite Psalm 44, at the end of which the psalmist says, "Rouse thyself! Why sleepest thou, O Lord? Awake! Do not cast us off forever! ... Rise up, come to our help!" Please join me in this prayer through the intercession of our two newly canonized Holy Popes.

Part 2

THE RELATIONSHIP BETWEEN RELIGIOUS AND ECONOMIC LIBERTY IN AN AGE OF EXPANDING GOVERNMENT

5

Preserving Religious Liberty in an Age of Expanding Government

Cardinal Robert Sarah

Introductory Remarks

It is with joy that I address this general theme concerning religious liberty in the face of expanding government. This is a topic of great importance in my service as president of the Pontifical Council *Cor Unum*. This dicastery of the Roman Curia was established in 1971 by the recently beatified Pope Paul VI. Reflecting the greatest of the Lord's commands—love of God and love of neighbor (Mark 12:29–31)—our office has been entrusted with the realization of the Holy Father's charitable intentions in the face of concrete needs, such as when natural disasters strike in the world. Our task is to encourage and coordinate the organizations and charitable activities promoted by the Catholic Church. "Coordination" is not limited to the technical and practical: We also work to foster the catechesis of charity through reflection on its source, origins, motives, methods, and ends; we do all of this with a view to supporting the faithful to give a concrete witness to evangelical charity. I was appointed president of *Cor Unum* in 2010, and, since then, I have gained a greater awareness of the charitable works and programs of Catholic organizations all over the world, as well as the challenges that they face in a rapidly changing environment.

Within the United States, we are well aware of numerous "witnesses of charity." I take this opportunity to express our gratitude to them: not only to those directly sponsored by the bishops, such as Catholic Charities USA and Catholic Relief Services but also to religious institutes and associations of Christian charity; to organizations for human development and missionary service; to groups involved in the civil sphere; and to organizations for social, educational, and cultural work. Many Catholic charitable institutions and structures have been founded to assist those in need. Many consecrated religious have spent their whole lives as witnesses of God's love in self-giving service. We are grateful that Americans generously give hundreds of billions of dollars each year to various charitable causes both on their own continent and abroad. In every corner of the world, they dedicate untold hours to voluntary service. Whether in the wake of the devastation wrought by Louisiana's Hurricane Katrina; the unprecedented destruction of Haiti's great earthquake; or in response to the never-ending cry of the war-ridden, refugee-provoking, and poverty-stricken regions of Africa and the Middle East, Americans of faith and no faith manifest an exemplary eagerness to help those in need. To all of you and to all the selfless individuals and organizations here in America who give of their time, talents, and treasure to care for those in need, in the name of the Church and our Holy Father, Pope Francis, I thank you.

The Church will always have a preferential love for the poor. It can never ignore the sufferings of increasing numbers of our brothers and sisters. This service of evangelical love has become an essential part of American culture. Yet in America, as in so many parts of the world, the ability of Catholic charitable organizations to hold on to this heritage and identity and to exercise their distinct mission is being threatened by restrictions to freedom and growing government control in an increasingly secular environment. On almost a daily basis, we hear of what religious minorities worldwide suffer simply because of their beliefs: merciless beheadings, bombings of churches, torching of orphanages, and ruthless expulsions of entire families from their homes. They are discriminated against in so many basic areas of human dignity: education, employment, housing, land ownership, and the legal recognition of marriages and births. According to a January 2014 Pew Research Center study, 75 percent of the world's population "live in countries where governments, social groups, or individuals restrict people's ability to freely practice their faith."[1] One third of the 198 countries surveyed had high religious hostilities (up from 20 percent in 2007), especially against

---

[1] "Religious Hostilities Reach Six-Year High," January 14, 2014, http://www.pewforum.org/2014/01/14/religious-hostilities-reach-six-year-high/.

Christians. Even today, brothers and sisters in the faith suffer persecution because they sign themselves with the cross, bow their heads at the Holy Name of Jesus, or happily profess the Apostles' Creed. Experts calculate that half of all Christian martyrs were killed in the twentieth century alone. Even in this still-young twenty-first century, one million people have been martyred around the world because of their belief in Jesus Christ.

Even in the great nation of the United States, religious freedom is being restricted and slowly eroded. Because this touches our theme and as president of the Holy See's office responsible for charity, I would like to direct my essay to the situation here, focusing on three distinct areas. First, what is the mission of Catholic charitable organizations and the Church's teaching on religious freedom? Second, how does the historical and current situation in the United States affect this mission? Third, how do we move forward in the situation in which we find ourselves, both in the United States and beyond?

THE MISSION OF CATHOLIC CHARITABLE ORGANIZATIONS AND THE CHURCH'S TEACHING ON RELIGIOUS FREEDOM

The Mission of Catholic Charitable Organizations

"God is love, and whoever remains in love remains in God and God in him" (1 John 4:16). In the words of Pope Emeritus Benedict XVI, these words express "with remarkable clarity the heart of the Christian faith."[2] This most central of Jesus' teachings underlines the importance of understanding the oneness of the Bible's two love commands. When one of the scribes asked, "Which is the first of all the commandments," Jesus replied, "The first is this: ... 'you shall love the Lord your God with all your heart'... The second is this: 'You shall love your neighbor as yourself.' There is no other commandment greater than these" (Mark 12:28–31). To begin to grasp the Church's ancient confession, "God is love," two actions are needed simultaneously: love of God and love of neighbor. They form a single commandment. Both live from the love of God who loved us first. They give rise to the concrete and organized expression of love in the Church—*caritas*—based on three fundamental tenets.

First, Christian charity is *anthropological*. In the creation account at the very beginning of sacred Scripture, God said, "Let us make human beings in our image, after our likeness" (Gen. 1:26). What is the "image and likeness"

---

[2] Pope Benedict XVI, Encyclical Letter *Deus Caritas Est* (2005), no. 1.

that we find in God? It is the love that we discover in the Trinity: a diversity of Persons—Father, Son, and Holy Spirit—who live in perfect unity. In this diversity and perfect unity, we perceive how the nature of God is love—perfect charity. Diversity necessarily implies otherness. It means relation, openness, and the gift of self to the other. In this otherness, only perfect charity—love that goes to the end—can create unity. Divine revelation also teaches how this intra-Trinitarian love is not imprisoned in the Godhead but reaches beyond itself in seeking out a relationship with the human person. Therefore, we are created in God's image and likeness to "love one another ... as I have loved you" (John 13:34). Hence, Christian charity not only makes *incarnate* the love of God that seeks out man in his concrete situation, but it also makes *present* God's willingness to pour himself out in love.

From this anthropological foundation of charity flows a second fundamental tenet: Christian charity is *ecclesial*. The practice of love—charitable activity (*diakonia*)—along with the proclamation of God's Word (*kerygma-martyria*) and the celebration of the sacraments (*leitourgia*), is a constitutive element of the Church's mission and an indispensable expression of its very being.[3] The Church exists in this world as the instrument of God's will: "His will was that men should have access to the Father through Christ, the Word made flesh, in the Holy Spirit, and thus become sharers in the divine nature."[4] Through the proclamation of the Word, the celebration of the sacraments, and the practice of charity, the Church carries out its mission to give all women and men access to and a share in the divine nature of the God who is love.

The mutual bond of the three ecclesial gifts (*munera*)—proclaiming God's Word, celebrating the sacraments, and exercising the ministry of charity—makes manifest the intrinsic bond between charity and evangelization and brings us to the third fundamental tenet of charity: its *missionary* character. Christian charity is not something that just responds to material needs. It is not a humanitarian endeavor to provide social assistance. Of course, when charity is placed before a need, it will strive to relieve it. But by its very nature, every work of charity bears a message of faith. Christian charity is permeated by the gospel and hence cannot be separated from the encounter with God. Through its practice, giver and receiver alike encounter the God of love and grow in relationship with him. Christian charity is the "human

---

[3] See Pope Benedict XVI, *Deus Caritas Est*, no. 25; and Pope Benedict XVI, *Motu Proprio Intima Ecclesiae Natura*, November 11, 2012.

[4] Second Vatican Council, *Dogmatic Constitution on Divine Revelation (Dei Verbum)*, 2n.

face" of God. "If you see charity, you see the Trinity," Augustine wrote.[5] In doing charity, Catholic charitable organizations become the sign of the Church and its most basic reason for existing: to proclaim by words and deeds the love that God has shown to the world in Jesus Christ. The witness to love becomes an apostle; in the witness of love, at least a seed of belief is sown even in those who do not believe or whose faith is weak.

The Church's Teaching on Religious Freedom

So important is this basic human right to the Church that the Second Vatican Council dedicated an entire landmark document to its treatment. The council fathers state that "the human person has a right to religious freedom," and call upon governments to "assume the safeguard of the religious freedom of all [their] citizens."[6] This freedom means that all men and women are to be immune from coercion on the part of individuals or of social groups or of any human power in such wise that in matters religious, no one is to be forced to act in a manner contrary to his or her own beliefs, whether privately or publicly, whether alone or in association with others. The right of every citizen to religious liberty and the responsibility of government to safeguard it was reiterated recently by Pope Francis who stated:

> the juridical, state and international regulations are called to recognize, guarantee and protect religious liberty, which is intrinsically inherent right to human nature, to its dignity of being free, and is also an indicator of a healthy democracy and one of the principal sources of the legitimacy of the State.[7]

An important distinction should be made here from the outset and particularly in nations where freedom is cherished so greatly, such as the United States. When the Church speaks about religious freedom, it is not arguing solely for freedom from coercion or persecution in matters of personal faith and conscience. Religious freedom is not only about worship, such as the liberty to go to Mass on Sunday or pray the rosary at home. It includes

---

[5] Augustine, *De Trinitate*, VIII, 8.

[6] Second Vatican Council, *Declaration on Religious Liberty* (*Dignitatis Humanae*), no. 6.

[7] Address to the International Congress organized by the Department of Jurisprudence of LUMSA and of St. John's School of Law on the subject: "Religious Liberty According to International Law and the Global Conflict of Values," Rome, June 20–21, 2014.

also the institutional freedom of the Church and religious organizations to provide education, health care, and other social services, and to contribute to the common good of all people. In his first encyclical, Saint John Paul II wrote that "freedom is a great gift ... Christ teaches us that the best use of freedom is charity, which takes concrete form in self-giving and in service."[8] Following on from this, Pope Francis writes that religious freedom

> includes "the freedom to choose the religion which one judges to be true and to manifest one's beliefs in public." A healthy pluralism, one which genuinely respects differences and values them as such, does not entail privatizing religions in an attempt to reduce them to the quiet obscurity of the individual's conscience or to relegate them to the enclosed precincts of churches, synagogues or mosques.[9]

The Situation in the United States: Historical and Actual

The Historical Situation

The history of Catholic charitable activity in what is now the United States extends all the way back to 1727, a generation before the American Revolution. Ursuline nuns arrived in Louisiana from France and founded an orphanage, hospital, and girls' school. Their service was largely to non-Catholics—Native Americans, slaves, and children from homes broken by alcohol and abuse.

The development of the sisters' relationship with the American government is key to understanding religious freedom for charitable institutions in the United States. At the time of the sisters' arrival, Louisiana belonged to the French. When, in 1803, the American government bought the territory from France, the nuns sought assurances from President Thomas Jefferson to protect the freedom with which they carried out their work. The president's response is of vital importance. He told the sisters that the principles of the American Constitution were a "sure guarantee" that their ministry would be free to "govern itself according to its own voluntary rules, without interference from the civil authority." Moreover, President Jefferson wrote that "whatever diversity of shade may appear in the religious opinions of our fellow citizens, the charitable objects of your institution ... and its

---

[8] Pope John Paul II, Encyclical Letter *Redemptor Hominis* (1979), no. 21.

[9] Pope Francis, Apostolic Exhortation *Evangelii Gaudium* (2013), no. 25.

furtherance of the wholesome purposes of society ... cannot fail to ensure it the patronage of the government it is under. Be assured that it will meet with all the protection which my office can give it."[10]

It seems to me that President Jefferson was making a fundamental assertion. America has a commitment to religious freedom based on the recognition that charitable institutions contribute to the "furtherance of the wholesome purposes of society." This is why Americans to this day consider it quite normal for religious charities, including Catholic ones, to make use of public monies in serving the poor, the sick, the homeless, immigrants, and other needy populations.

The Actual Situation

In recent years, we hear that the freedom of charitable institutions in this nation to provide services according to their religious beliefs is being eroded. More and more, religious entities find themselves restricted by civil authorities—through the courts, legislatures, and federal and state bureaucracies—who seek to dictate the terms under which they provide their services. In terms of Catholic organizations, this threatens the character and mission of charity, which we have shown to be based on three fundamental tenets—anthropological, ecclesial, and missionary.

Consider two lamentable examples. In the past, some local chapters of Catholic Charities, such as Boston, San Francisco, the District of Columbia, and the state of Illinois, contracted with civil authority to provide foster care and adoption services. But in recent times, civil authority through its own legislation has tried to pressure Catholic adoption agencies to place children with same-sex couples—a clear violation of the Church's teachings on marriage, sexuality, and the human person—going as far as revoking their licenses and ending their government contracts. Catholic charitable agencies are given the choice to comply or withdraw from the adoption service. Even more recently, this nation has witnessed an unprecedented attack on religious freedom in the form of the mandate of the Department of Health and Human Services (the "HHS mandate") by which the government forces religious institutions to facilitate and fund products—contraception, sterilization, and abortion-inducing drugs—contrary to their own moral teachings and undermining the right of conscientious objection. There are

---

[10] John Gilmary Shea, *Life and Times of the Most Rev. John Carroll* (New York: John G. Shea, 1888), 588–89.

many other examples of this creeping attack on religious freedom ranging from discrimination against small church congregations and Christian students on university campuses to immigration laws in states throughout the United States.

For many of us outside the United States, such a trend is not only alarming but also puzzling on at least two levels. First, the heritage of religious liberty in this nation—the most cherished of American freedoms—has enabled people of faith to contribute to their communities; in the words of President Jefferson, to contribute to the "furtherance of the wholesome purposes of society." So we see how an impressive array of charitable endeavors has blossomed here in favor of orphans, immigrants, ethnic groups, and all people in need: programs of health care for the elderly and disabled; work with the sick and disadvantaged; assistance to families and expectant mothers; and initiatives to feed, clothe, and legally protect the poor. Catholic Charities USA, for example, is one of the largest private nongovernmental charitable networks in the nation, with distinctly low overheads and dedicated staff. Even if the government wished to assume all outreach itself, it would take years to replace Church charities with government-run programs. This selfless service, which has become an essential characteristic of American culture, is nurtured by faith and enriches public life. It reflects also the notion of *subsidiarity*, a core principle of Catholic social teaching. Through mediating institutions such as the Church, America has always sought to meet people's needs at both a local and a personal level, thereby keeping government properly limited. Indeed, government can never love one's neighbor as one's self. It has no soul and heart. That is why your nation has allowed living and mediating forces, such as the Church, to offer not only material help but also refreshment and care for their souls, which often is even more necessary than material support.

Second, your nation is built on a set of moral claims about God, the human person, the meaning of life, and the purpose of society, which were given by America's first settlers and founders. How well known it is that God is named in your founding documents as "Creator" and "Supreme Judge" over individuals and governments. The human person is said to be endowed with God-given and therefore inalienable rights to "life, liberty, and the pursuit of happiness." The purpose of government is clearly defined and sharply limited: to help secure and defend these basic rights for its citizens. James Madison, often called the Father of the Constitution, described conscience as "the most sacred of all property."[11] George Washington wrote that "the establishment of Civil and Religious Liberty was the motive that induced me to the field of battle."[12] When the Bill of Rights was ratified, religious freedom had the distinction of being the First Amendment. Indeed, the First Amendment guarantees that "Congress shall make no law respecting an establishment or religion, or prohibiting the free exercise thereof." The American ideal resembles Lord Acton's famous definition of freedom: "not the power of doing what we like, but the right of being able to do what we ought."[13] This is quite different to much of Europe, where the rise of the nation state led to a hostile and anticlerical attitude to religion. In America, religion was seen as a key ingredient to promoting the good of the citizens. Church and state were kept separate to guarantee that citizens could worship freely and practice their faith without government interference.

All of this is compounded by an underlying philosophy in society of aggressive and reductionist secularism that seeks to exclude the role of religion in public life and, as a result, sets up a culture without God, wherein everyone can live without the law of truth and love engraved by the Creator God upon the heart of every human being. Secularism seeks to substitute God and his law with personal opinions, ideologies, pleasures, and needs. In this worldview, each person should have as much freedom as possible to pursue the good as he sees it. Moreover, government, both at the federal and the state levels, is growing so big that it regulates even the freedom to practice the faith. The danger is this: When God is taken out and religion gets crowded into a corner by government expansion, with citizens forced to put aside their religious convictions, society not only excludes the great contribution of religion but also promotes a culture that redefines man as less than what he is. Pope Francis has described this underlying philosophy as a "sickness":

> Religious liberty is not only that of thought or private worship. It is freedom to live according to ethical principles consequent upon the truth found, be it privately or publicly. This is a great challenge in the

---

[11] James Madison, "Property," *National Gazette*, March 29, 1792.

[12] Michael Novak and Jana Novak, *Washington's God* (New York: Basic Books, 2006), 111.

[13] Lord John Acton, "The Roman Question," *The Rambler* (January 1860): 146. See also John Courtney Murray, *We Hold These Truths: Catholic Reflections on the American Proposition* (1960; repr., New York: Sheed & Ward, 1988), chap. 1.

globalized world, where weak thought—which is like a sickness—also lowers the general ethical level, and in the name of a false concept of tolerance ends up by persecuting those who defend the truth about man and the ethical consequences.[14]

The Response

We have thus far considered two important areas. First, we discussed the character and mission of Catholic charitable organizations, which we proposed as based on three fundamental tenets—anthropological, ecclesial, and missionary. As part of this discussion, we reviewed also the Church's teaching on religious freedom. In our second major area, we grounded ourselves firmly in the historical perspective to survey the situation in which these organizations find themselves in the face of expanding government and aggressive secularism. In this final section, I would like to suggest the response that is needed to defend religious liberty by offering three simple suggestions.

Pray

Our first task is to pray for the current situation and to encourage intercession. A beautiful exhortation in this direction is given by Pope Benedict in *Deus Caritas Est*: "Prayer, as a means of drawing ever new strength from Christ, is concretely and urgently needed. People who pray are not wasting their time, even though the situation appears desperate and seems to call for action alone."[15]

We might remember how prayers for "the conversion of Russia" at the end of many a Mass over a half-century ago shaped our sense of what was going on behind the Iron Curtain and perhaps even curtailed Communism. More recently, we witnessed and perhaps even participated in Pope Francis's call for prayer and fasting to end the chemical weapons' crisis in Syria, which undoubtedly contributed to the end of immediate hostilities. On that September evening in Saint Peter's Square, at which I, too, was present, tens

---

[14] Address given to the International Congress, Department of Jurisprudence of LUMSA, Rome, June 20–21, 2014.

[15] Benedict XVI, *Deus Caritas Est*, no. 36.

of thousands came and millions across the planet joined in local gatherings.[16] Prayer is powerful and heightens awareness of the challenges that we face.

In terms of our Catholic charitable organizations and those who serve in them, prayer also means that we draw from the primordial source of divine Charity—God himself—in order that we can love as he has loved us. I am convinced that the best way to protect religious freedom is to remind ourselves and others that we should first love God. This happens only in prolonged moments of prayer, listening to the Word of God, receiving the sacraments, and adoring Jesus in the Eucharist, the source and summit of the Christian life.

During his homily to the cardinal electors at the beginning of his pontificate, Pope Francis warned us about the direction that the Church takes when reference to Jesus Christ is lacking: "We may become a charitable NGO, but not the Church, the bride of the Lord."[17] The great saints of Christian charity in this nation burned with love for our crucified and risen Lord Jesus Christ and drew their own witness from his saving act of love *to the end* on the cross. Just think of St. Elizabeth Ann Seton's educational mission to the poor and underprivileged, St. Frances Cabrini's tireless efforts on behalf of defenseless immigrants, and St. Katharine Drexel's concern for the oppressed Native Americans and blacks. Whatever the challenges of an increasingly encroaching government apparatus or the aggressive secularism of society, if we return constantly to God in our own personal lives and organizations, then all our charitable activities realized in the name of the Church will endure because "love never fails" (1 Cor. 13:8).

Uphold Catholic Identity

Second, we need to look for ways to uphold the Catholic character of our charitable organizations. One very concrete reason for the erosion of religious freedom is that we are becoming increasingly lukewarm in our beliefs. In many historically Catholic countries of Europe, the Church risks irrelevance. In France, once known as the "eldest daughter of the Church," only 4.5 percent of Catholics go to Mass weekly—down from 27 percent

---

[16] "Pope Francis at Angelus: Sept 7 Day of Prayer for Peace," News.va, http://www.news.va/en/news/pope-francis-at-angelus-sept-7-day-of-prayer-for-p.

[17] Homily of the Holy Father Pope Francis, "Missa Pro Ecclesia" with the Cardinal Electors, 14 March 2013, http://w2.vatican.va/content/francesco/en/homilies/2013/documents/papa-francesco_20130314_omelia-cardinali.html.

in 1965. Americans, too, are measurably less religious than a few decades ago. In a recently published book, Charles Murray reports that amongst white working-class Americans, the number of people who profess no religion or attend a worship service no more than once a year has gone up from 38 percent to 59 percent. A similar trend is registered in marriage commitment and out-of-wedlock births.[18] We need to be clear: Society will not care about religious freedom if it does not care about God. The best way to protect religious freedom is to bring people back to faith with love of God and neighbor.

This is why I believe that charity offers a unique "visitor's card" into evangelization. Christian charity does not seek to proselytize, yet many of those we serve either may not believe or may have a weak faith. Every charitable act carries within it an encounter with God, and our organizations and their personnel need to be permeated with a Christian spirit so that our outreach *ad extra* is first nurtured within ourselves *ad intra*.

What do I mean by this? In recent years and following the directives given by Pope Benedict XVI,[19] our dicastery *Cor Unum* has placed great emphasis on a "formation of the heart." This implies evangelizing our very selves within charitable entities, allowing the gospel to penetrate our sentiments and our thoughts so that our work reveals the God who has first loved us (1 John 4:10). This is a point we would do well to reflect on. What can we do in our organizations to link together charity and evangelization in the life of those who work for us? Of course, this requires hiring Catholics who are personally engaged, articulate, and well-informed with the courage and critical skills to articulate the integral Christian vision of the human person—body and soul—as he or she relates to God in the face of an increasingly reductive view of man and woman and their complementarity. No Catholic ministry can expect to uphold its Catholic identity if key personnel are not Catholic.

Defend the Mission of Catholic Charity

Third, we must be resolute in upholding and defending the character and mission of Catholic charity. Faced with current challenges in our service to the poor, we may be tempted to change our principles—to compromise and give in. From the outset, I wish to say: Christian values—the anthropologi-

---

[18] Charles Murray, *Coming Apart: The State of White America 1960–2010* (Washington, DC: Crown Forum 2012).

[19] Benedict XVI, *Deus Caritas Est*, no. 31a.

cal, ecclesial, and missionary foundations of Catholic charitable organizations—are nonnegotiable. As such, any ideology contrary to the teaching of the Lord as transmitted by the Church and any financial aid that imposes ideological conditions opposed to the magisterium must be rejected categorically. We cannot let ourselves be absorbed by those who, with powerful means—whether financial or of the mass media with a great manipulative capacity—seek to spread a philosophy of so-called rights that damages and even destroys the Christian vision of the human person, created in the image and likeness of God, and called to a heavenly destiny. As a result, the Christian mission of charity and love for the poor must continue in the reflection of Christ's greatest command to love God and neighbor—with or without the financial support of the government and *never* at the cost of Catholic identity. As Blessed Teresa of Calcutta once said so wisely: "The others do good because of something. We do good because of Someone." Being faithful to this Someone—God himself—may bring exclusion and even persecution as Jesus told us in the beginning: "Whoever wishes to come after me must deny himself, take up his cross, and follow me" (Matt.16:24).

Surely, the current difficult circumstances of restrictions on religious liberty present an obstacle to freely realize the Church's mission of charity. They also offer an exceptional occasion to go back to the roots of our Catholic identity. Thus, our Catholic identity, besides being a challenge, is also a gateway to renewal for our charitable institutions. Tapping into our Catholic roots becomes a source of renewal for Catholic charitable organizations and helps us rediscover and appreciate this great treasure—our Catholic faith and tradition. Today, the Church and our charitable agencies have a mission to civil society based on being true to who we are: to repropose the question of faith, the centrality of the human person, and life and family within the public debate so that charity can offer its contribution and orientation, lest the world succumb to a dehumanized logic. The consequences of an unbridled and aggressive secularism are all too evident. They produce a "culture of death," where we become accustomed to growing numbers of abortions, marital breakdowns, euthanasia, suicides, the taking of life through senseless acts of violence and terrorism, and the decline in the birthrate. The divine gift of love-to-the-end shows itself to be the decisive factor in the restoration of human dignity by proclaiming and giving witness to the love of Christ. This is the great mission before us.

Conclusion

To be Catholic and a good citizen should mean not having to choose one over the other. Allegiances are distinct, but they need not be contradictory and should instead be complementary. This is the teaching of the Church, which obliges us to work together for the common good. It is also the vision of the founding and Constitution of this great nation, which guarantees citizens of all religious faiths the right to contribute to your common life together. Without religious freedom properly understood, all suffer, deprived of the essential contribution in education, health care, feeding the hungry, civil rights, and social services that religious people make every day, both in the United States and overseas. Moreover, if we are not free in our conscience and our practice of religion, all other freedoms become fragile and futile.

Perhaps the great patron of religious liberty, Saint Thomas More, can teach us how to move forward. As chancellor to King Henry VIII, he yearned to serve both God and king as well as he could and for as long as he could. The saint used his God-given intelligence, prudence, and creativity in expending every last effort not to die but to live—for his family; for his faith; and yes, for king and country. In this moment of history, we, too, are called to seek ways to defend, preserve, and pass on the blessings of freedom that the founders of this nation secured, thus helping the United States truly become a land of the free and a beacon of hope both here and for so many other lands where believers suffer even death from restrictions to religious freedom.

In the end, Saint Thomas More chose martyrdom over any constraint imposed on his God-given conscience—even by the king of England. He died proclaiming that he was "the King's good servant, but God's first." He gave his life in the supreme sacrifice because he first loved God and sought selflessly the salvation of his neighbor's soul.

6

RELIGIOUS AND ECONOMIC LIBERTY AND AMERICA'S FOUNDING

Michael Novak

Religious liberty and economic liberty are intimately related. Religious liberty is more basic and gives deeper grounding to all other freedoms. Economic liberty is both one of the natural fruits of religious liberty and one of its enabling conditions. Without economic liberty, religious liberty cannot fully flower.

Religion sets profound duties on both body and soul. To fulfill those duties, economic freedom is a necessary means. Economic freedom amplifies the flourishing of religion.

RELIGIOUS LIBERTY

From "Duty" to "Right"

The most direct path to understanding a natural right to religious liberty is by way of a Christian philosophy. There are other paths but none so direct. In any case, that is the path taken by Thomas Jefferson and James Madison in putting a foundation under their claim of a natural right to religious liberty. If anyone wishes to follow another path, he must mark it out and show that it works better, or at least as well. For Jefferson and Madison (and for myself), the Christian way works best. It is shortest and easiest to understand for the largest public: Religious freedom is grounded in the *duty* of a human being to give gratitude to and worship its Creator. No duty is prior to that one.

Why "to give gratitude"? Because without the Creator, the creature would not exist. The creature owes all she is and has to her Creator. Not to fulfill that duty is to show herself an ingrate.

Why worship? Because the gap between the Creator and the creature is infinite, and basic honesty calls for grateful acknowledgment of that gap with wonder and awe.

Imagine for example the delightful range of Mozart's music and Vivaldi's and Beethoven's and Handel's and Dvorak's. Then think of the Creator who empowered each of them. If it is true that whatever is achieved by humans is first conceived in the fertile mind of the Creator, what infinite ranges of music resound within him?

We can also bring to mind the stunningly beautiful sunsets over lakes, seas, and prairies that we have seen. Remember their variety day after day, year after year. Is not the most delightful and most frequent way to God through beauty?

That is why the right to religious liberty—the right to liberty of conscience—begins in a duty of gratitude and a duty of honest recognition of the infinite gap between humans and God.

The American Contribution

How is it that James Madison and Thomas Jefferson—to cite authorities from our own land—came to call religious freedom a *right*? For the reason that if humans have a duty to worship and to give thanks to their creator, no one else dares to interfere with their fulfilling that right. No one dares step between his creatures and their Creator. That special duty creates an inalienable right.

Our founders thought such a duty to be self-evident. Any man who recognizes the gap between the Creator and himself immediately recognizes his duty to give thanks and, more than that, to worship. So great is the gap between creature and Creator that gratitude and awe are the one appropriate response. True religion, Rudolf Otto wrote, springs from "fear and trembling."[1] With the Jewish and the Christian God in mind, amazement and love seem more appropriate.

---

[1] Rudolf Otto, *The Idea of the Holy: An Inquiry into the Non-rational Factor in the Idea of the Divine and Its Relation to the Rational*, trans. John W. Harvey (1920; repr., London: Oxford University Press, 1923).

The right to religious liberty is inalienable. It is inalienable, first, from the side of God, because it springs from a duty owed to him. These duties to God are prior to all other duties—they are prior to government, prior to civil society, and prior to the authority of parents, peers, and friends.

This right is inalienable, also, from the side of man because only the individual person can meet that duty—no one else, no other. Only the individual subject can fulfill his duty to his Creator. His parents and friends cannot meet this duty for him. His government cannot fulfill it.

Almighty God, although he was under no obligation to do so, created the human person *free*. God offers human beings his friendship, but he does not want the friendship of slaves and the prostrations and submission of slaves. He wants the friendship of free persons standing erect.

What if someone denies that man is a religious animal? What if a significant minority denies that there is any creator at all? Can the right to religious freedom be defended in such a situation? Does one need to argue the prior question of anthropology first? This, I think, is putting the burden on the wrong party.

Perhaps those who deny that there is a creator, or even a God who is not a creator but merely the first intelligent cause of the universe like that of Aristotle and Plato, actually have no justification for respecting religious liberty. Or perhaps they have only a restricted list of those eligible for such a liberty. John Locke, for instance, denied it to atheists and Catholics.[2] In any case, the atheistic regimes of the twentieth century denied such liberty altogether and had few qualms about putting to death those they wished to. That fills most Americans with revulsion. But why? How do they ground their right to freedom of conscience?

Hobbes has one answer, but it has its own problems. Locke has another, but it is not quite adequate either. A pluralism of reasons for honoring liberty of conscience is probably a good thing, but a systematic relativism is fatal to religious liberty. It has led in the past hundred years to at least two dictatorships of relativism.

It may help to meditate on the full concept of liberty employed in the principle of religious liberty—or for those who so prefer, liberty of conscience.

---

[2] See John Locke, *A Letter Concerning Toleration* (1689).

A Fresh Understanding of Liberty

Let us allow a great French poet to express the joy that the Creator takes in the freedom of his human persons. Then we shall hear how Jefferson and Madison expressed it.

First, Charles Peguy:

> *Such is the mystery of man's freedom.*
> *Such is the price we set on man's freedom.*
> *Because I myself am free, says God, and I have created man*
>   *in my own image and likeness....*
> *That freedom of that creature is the most beautiful reflection*
>   *in this world*
> *Of the Creator's freedom....*
>
> *A salvation that was not free, that was not, that did not come*
>   *from a free man could in no wise be attractive to us.*
>   *What would it amount to?*
> *What would it mean?*
> *What interest would such a salvation have to offer?*
> *A beatitude of slaves, a salvation of slaves, a slavish beatitude,*
>   *how do you expect me to be interested in that kind of thing?*
>   *Does one care to be loved by slaves?*
>
> *When you once have known what it is to be loved freely,*
>   *submission no longer has any taste.*
> *All the prostrations in the world*
> *Are not worth the beautiful upright attitude of a free man as he kneels.*
>   *All the submission, all the dejections in the world*
> *Are not equal in value to the soaring up point,*
> *The beautiful straight soaring up of one single invocation*
> *From a love that is free.*[3]

Second, Thomas Jefferson:

> Well aware that Almighty God hath created the mind free; that all attempts to influence it by temporal punishments or burthens, or by civil incapacitations, tend only to beget habits of hypocrisy and meanness, and are a departure from the plan of the Holy Author of our religion,

---

[3] Excerpt from Charles Péguy, "Freedom," trans. Ann and Julian Green, http://allpoetry.com/poem/8533051-Freedom-by-Charles-Peguy.

who being Lord both of body and mind, yet chose not to propagate it by coercions on either, as was in his Almighty power to do.[4]

Third, James Madison:

> Because we hold it for a fundamental and undeniable truth, "that religion or the duty which we owe to our Creator and the manner of discharging it, can be directed only by reason and conviction, not by force or violence," The Religion then of every man must be left to the conviction and conscience of every man; and it is the right of every man to exercise it as these may dictate.
>
> Whilst we assert for ourselves a freedom to embrace, to profess and to observe the Religion which we believe to be of divine origin, we cannot deny an equal freedom to those whose minds have not yet yielded to the evidence which has convinced us. If this freedom be abused, it is an offence against God, not against man: To God, therefore, not to man, must an account of it be rendered.[5]

Therefore, it is clear for our founders that religious freedom is begotten by a duty to the Creator. Duties to the Creator are the source of human rights. Such duties are what make rights sacred, that is, more than simply human conventions.

Two points are worth stressing. First, although the first right of religious liberty is articulated initially in political documents, these documents actually point out that religious liberty is a prepolitical, natural right. The right to religious liberty "is endowed in us by our Creator"; not by any other source—neither state nor civil society.

Second, one of the most beautiful aspects of looking at religious freedom this way (at bottom a way suggested by Christian concepts of God and man, as Jefferson and Madison confess) is that the principle of religious liberty, or perhaps better here, liberty of conscience, cannot be held true only for believers in a creator. Such a liberty, founded only on the evidence presented to the reasoned inquiry and reflection of one person and then another, must belong to all humans, not only to the religious person but also to the unbeliever. Thus Madison: "We cannot deny an equal freedom to those whose minds have not yet yielded to the evidence which has convinced us."

---

[4] Thomas Jefferson, *The Virginia Act for Establishing Religious Freedom* (1786).

[5] James Madison, *Memorial and Remonstrance against Religious Assessments* (1785).

Oddly enough, one finds this generous way of regarding liberty of conscience virtually only in thinkers of a marked Christian inspiration. John Locke, as noted earlier, denied such liberty to atheists and to Catholics. The early John Rawls disqualified Christians and other believers from open access to the public square, limiting admission to the latter only to atheists, agnostics, and doubters.[6] He was, for a time and uncharacteristically, intolerant of reasoning nourished by religious faith.

This intolerance flies in the face of the historical correlation noticed by the great historian of liberty, Lord Acton, whose exhaustive findings may be summarized by the claim that the history of liberty is coincident with Christianity.[7] Christian faith must be approached with inquiring reason. The first principle of Christian teaching is this: "In the beginning was the Word [Logos], and the Word was with God, and the Word was God" (John 1:1). That declaration grounds both the nature of God and the nature of humans in Logos—reason, understanding, insight, reflective judgment, law. The Christian faith must be approached by way of the inquiring conscience of each person.

That historical point may explain why in the contemporary period (the last two hundred years), Christians have found it far easier to tolerate atheists, agnostics, and doubters than the latter have to tolerate Christians.[8] In no age of history have so many Christians been tortured for holding to their faith, forced to recant under threat of death, and summarily put to death.[9] The bloodiest century for the Church has fallen during the so-called Age of Reason and Enlightenment.[10]

We turn now to economic liberty.

---

[6] See John Rawls, *Political Liberalism* (New York: Columbia University Press, 1993).

[7] Only Christian concepts of God and man have given rise to cultures of full human liberty. See Michael Novak, "Seven Whig Amendments to the Liberal Theory of Liberty," in *On Cultivating Liberty: Reflections on Moral Ecology*, ed. Brian C. Anderson (Lanham, MD: Rowman & Littlefield, 1999), 37.

[8] Cf. Phillipe Benéton, "True and False Tolerance," in *A Free Society Reader: Principles for the New Millennium*, ed. Michael Novak, William Brailsford, and Cornelius Heesters (Lanham, MD: Lexington Books, 2000), 231–36.

[9] Cf. Robert Royal, *The Christian Martyrs of the Twentieth Century* (New York: Crossroad Publishing, 2000).

[10] One still duly notes the comments of Pope Benedict, inter alia, on the thorough compatibility of reason and faith. See, for example, the penultimate paragraph of his

THE THREE RIGHTS OF ECONOMIC LIBERTY

The Historical Case for Private Property

An important historical correlation was first observed many centuries ago: when all economic activity is communal or collective and when private property and private initiative are repressed, then the heavy burden of labor leads many persons to do as little as they can get away with. Further, even the highly motivated see the pointlessness of extra effort. In Plymouth Colony that first winter, the winter of communal labor, the whole colony came close to starvation. After that, respect for private property and personal initiative were restored, and steady growth ensued.[11]

Aristotle had written of this recurrent behavior already in the fourth century BC,[12] and Caesar recorded it in his accounts of poor agricultural results

---

Regensburg Address (September 12, 2006), http://www.vatican.va/holy_father/benedict_xvi/speeches/2006/september/documents/hf_ben-xvi_spe_20060912_university-regensburg_en.html:

> This attempt ... at a critique of modern reason from within has nothing to do with putting the clock back to the time before the Enlightenment and rejecting the insights of the modern age. The positive aspects of modernity are to be acknowledged unreservedly: We are all grateful for the marvelous possibilities that it has opened up for mankind and for the progress in humanity that has been granted to us. The scientific ethos, moreover, is ... the will to be obedient to the truth, and, as such, it embodies an attitude which belongs to the essential decisions of the Christian spirit. The intention here is not one of retrenchment or negative criticism, but of broadening our concept of reason and its application. While we rejoice in the new possibilities open to humanity, we also see the dangers arising from these possibilities and we must ask ourselves how we can overcome them. We will succeed in doing so only if reason and faith come together in a new way, if we overcome the self-imposed limitation of reason to the empirically falsifiable, and if we once more disclose its vast horizons. In this sense theology rightly belongs in the university and within the wide-ranging dialogue of sciences, not merely as a historical discipline and one of the human sciences, but precisely as theology, as inquiry into the rationality of faith.

[11] See Daniel J. Flynn, "Socialism Didn't Work at Plymouth Plantation, Either," *Human Events*, November 25, 2010, http://humanevents.com/2010/11/25/socialism-didnt-work-at-plymouth-plantation-either/.

[12] Cf. Aristotle, *Politics* 2.1–5.

among communal Germanic tribes.[13] Thus, serious men early concluded that it is better for the common good if a regime of private property is protected.

This was not an abstract point. It arose from and was confirmed by experience, and it is in line with common sense. The principle of private property is closely aligned with observable traits of human nature. This principle is written into natural law by the evidence of historical experience and is inscribed by way of historical experience among the natural rights of human beings.

Thus, from ancient times it was known that human nature carried in itself a right to private property. To interfere in that right would injure the *common* good, as well as injure a *person*'s ability to live up to his own individual potential. The Bible itself recognized the right to private property, when the seventh commandment set forth the prohibition: "Thou shalt not steal." The Catholic Church embraced that commandment, and relatively soon began emphasizing the natural right to the personal ownership of property. The reason offered was that this right better served the common good.

Under the general title "economic liberty" three human rights are respected: the right to private property, the right to *freedom of association*, and the right of the inventor to *the fruits of inventions of the human mind*. To the second of these we now turn.

The Right of Free Association

In the thirteenth century, Thomas Aquinas was the first to articulate the power of the right to association, empirically vindicated by its contributions to the common good. He gave a defense of the mendicant orders (and, more generally, other human associations) as potent contributors to the common good. In his *Contra Impugnantes* (1256), we read:

> In all social matters, the companionship of others is of great advantage. "A brother that is helped by his brother is like a strong city," says Solomon (Prov. xviii. 19). "It is better, therefore, that two should be together than one: for they have the advantage of their society" (Eccles. iv. 9).... Again, any person who is competent to perform some special function has a right to be admitted to the society of those who are selected for the exercise of that function. For, an association means the union of men, gathered together for the accomplishment of some specific work.[14]

---

[13] Cf. Julius Caesar, *Commentaries on the Gallic War*, bks. 4 and 6.

[14] St. Thomas Aquinas, *Liber Contra Impugnantes Dei Cultum et Religionem*, chap. 2.

Thus, the right of association, too, sprang from the nature of humans as social animals. Across Europe, more and more towns incorporated themselves in a kind of juridical association, and were awarded certain rights and liberties through charters granted by emperors, kings, or lesser political authorities. Guilds, sodalities, and associations of virtually all kinds, and in virtually all fields, flourished and became the very sinews that gave a workable structure to Western societies and Western liberties. For some centuries, Western societies were not ruled from the top down but by local customs and local institutions—primarily social associations. Nation-states were weak and disunited. Local associations flourished.

The Right to Patents and Copyrights

It took until more recent times, however, for a third newly recognized economic right to be singled out for protection: the right of authors and inventors to the fruits of their creations.[15]

This newly recognized right generated the explosion of intense activities of economic invention and creation that steadily enriched the whole of the North American continent. In turn, the success of America in raising up its immigrant poor into unparalleled affluence caught the world's attention through a host of European visitors, from the preeminent Alexis de Tocqueville to our virtual contemporaries Jacques Maritain (*Reflections on America*) and Jean-Jacques Servan-Schreiber (*The American Challenge*).[16]

One result of this rapid economic success created a new problem for Europe: *das Sozialproblem*.[17] How could France now explain the vast proportion of *les misérables* in its midst? Before America's thrust forward, it had been assumed that the poor would always be with us (Matt. 26:11). Now Europe's comparative poverty seemed inexcusable—a scandalous and massive failure. Some began shouting aloud the need for "revolution." Most of those who did so failed to grasp the actual causes of the wealth of nations

---

[15] See the patent and copyright clause of the US Constitution: Article 1, section 8. While the United Kingdom claims the longest continuous patent tradition dating back to the fifteenth century, in the United Kingdom patents were awarded by the Crown. In the United States, by contrast, the right inhered in the inventor, and the role of the Patent Office was merely to assure that proper conditions were met.

[16] Jacques Maritain, *Reflections on America* (New York: Charles Scribner's Sons, 1958); Jean-Jacques Servan-Schreiber, *The American Challenge*, trans. Ronald Steel (London: Hamish Hamilton, 1968).

[17] Cf. Hannah Arendt, *On Revolution* (New York: Viking, 1963).

and the economic liberties necessary for their flourishing. Their vision of progress proved in time to be most regressive.

The most dramatic result of the patent and copyright clause is that it changed the meaning of wealth. Until that time, the most prominent form of wealth had been land; physical property. Owners of enough land could assure themselves plenty of food and drink, even for a large retinue of courtiers and soldiers, as well as the national wherewithal to trade and barter at home and abroad.

Now a new form of wealth became real: *property in ideas*. This property in patents and copyrights gave rise to new forms of investment and production and then to the creative organization of society for invention, manufacturing, and worldwide trade. This massive societal shift not only caused much strain in society but also began almost immediately producing never before seen benefits for the poor—not only for upward mobility and steadily higher standards of living but preeminently in medical health, longevity, the relief of pain, and release from age-old diseases.

Abraham Lincoln Saw It Happening

Already in 1859, far out on America's western frontier at that time, Abraham Lincoln contemplated the planetary circulation of overseas goods that reached even the frontier communities of Illinois.

"Look around at Young America," Lincoln wrote in 1859. "Look at his apparel, and you shall see cotton fabrics from Manchester and Lowell, flax-linen from Ireland, wool-cloth from Spain, silk from France, furs from the Arctic regions, with a buffalo robe from the Rocky Mountains."[18] On Young America's table, one can find:

> Besides plain bread and meat made at home ... sugar from Louisiana, coffee and fruits from the tropics, salt from Turk's Island, fish from Newfoundland, tea from China, and spices from the Indies. The whale of the Pacific furnishes his candle-light, he has a diamond-ring from Brazil, a gold-watch from California, and a spanish cigar from Havanna.[19]

In short, the Agrarian Age that had lasted for two millennia began giving way to a new age—the Age of Manufacturing, Transport, and International

---

[18] Quoted in Michael Novak, *The Fire of Invention: Civil Society and the Future of the Corporation* (Lanham, MD: Rowman & Littlefield, 1997), 54–55.

[19] Novak, *The Fire of Invention*, 55.

Trade. With the invention and patenting of new means of instantaneous communication, transport, financial instruments, and the rapidity and the scope of trade, observers began speaking of "globalization," even though that process had been underway at slower speeds for centuries.

Thus it has come about that there is a new form of wealth far more versatile and transformative than land: namely, insights, ideas, inventions, and brainpower of the most extraordinary range and reach. The most significant form of capital is now no longer land, nor machinery, nor piles of gold—mere things—but, rather, *human capital*. That is, knowledge, know-how, creative skills, habits of discovery, and knowledge of how to organize new productive processes and to motivate alert and inventive and intensely cooperative persons.

The Catholic Church has come to recognize this huge transformation in the economics of human life, and its immense potential for improving the human condition of all the peoples on earth.[20] What it has been slower to recognize, however, is the root of this massive reconstruction of the social order, called for by Leo XIII in *Rerum Novarum*. The root of this transformation is economic liberty: economic liberty to invent, to take initiative, to create.

The impact of these fruits of economic liberty on religious liberty has been immense. Experience has shown that economic freedom is necessary if humans are to survive, prosper, and have the wherewithal to practice and spread their religious faith. Economic freedom also has crucial moral effects. It accustoms entire populations to show initiative, to think creatively, to take responsibility, to concern themselves with the common good of the entire human family, and to attend to *achieved results* (not solely to good intentions). In general, economic freedom encourages both a more inward self-accounting (current practices are always under review for improvement), and a more outward-extending community of concern (each firm is being habituated to think of serving not only its current markets but the whole world).

With economic liberty, newspapers in formerly Soviet countries could again purchase their own newsprint without worrying about punitive interruptions of supply by the state. The words of the Holy Father—and the daily parables of his actions caught on television—instantly reach the whole mystical body spread all around the globe, and allow him daily to preach also to the unconverted. The intense sufferings of the persecuted all around the globe are brought to instant attention. Swift transport of assistance to

---

[20] See Pope John Paul II, Encyclical Letter *Centesimus Annus* (1991).

the poor and the needy and to those struck by natural or human disaster is now possible. The works of religion are vastly enabled, beyond what was possible in earlier centuries. Corporal and spiritual works of mercy are rendered far more instantaneous and efficacious. The realm of religiously motivated action is vastly increased.

In a word, economic liberty produces fruits that give religiously conceived works of mercy a vaster field of freedom in which to act. Economic liberty and religious liberty benefit from each other and need each other.

Like religious freedom, economic liberty has its roots in the duty of human persons to their Creator. In this case, the duty of each human is to live up to the potential that God has written into his or nature—the potential to become creative as he is creative and to weave together all humankind in a form of international solidarity.

THE TWO LIBERTIES TOGETHER

Religious liberty is a natural right. Indeed, it is the first and most fundamental of natural rights from which all others spring. The American founders recognized that once a person recognizes the full meaning of *creature* and *Creator*, he recognizes as self-evident the duty in conscience of the former to the latter. He recognizes as well that this duty is inalienable. For Christians at least, such a ground for religious liberty means that the right of conscience extends to all persons, even to those who have not yet seen evidence for recognizing a Creator.

Economic liberty, as we have seen, is indispensable for allowing human persons to fulfill the creative impulse in our nature, felt even by those who do not admit that we are made in the image of the Creator of all things. The historical evidence is clear and inarguable.

Systems that respect and promote economic liberty are far more creative, habitually inventive, and self-improving. Best of all, they produce the best results, both for individual persons and for the common good.

Thus, religious freedom and economic freedom are intimately related. Religious freedom is deeper and more basic, and gives a more granite grounding to all other freedoms.

Economic freedom is also necessary, however, if humans are to survive, prosper, and have the wherewithal to practice and spread their religious faith. Economic freedom also accustoms entire populations to show initiative, to think creatively, to take responsibility, to concern themselves with results rather than intentions alone. In general, economic freedom encourages both a more inward self-accounting (What can we do better? How can we improve?) and a more outward-extending community of concern, which in its full development includes the whole human race, leaving nobody out.

In a time such as ours of ever-expanding and unlimited government, launched in the name of fulfilling the material needs of all citizens—an era that Tocqueville foresaw in his reflections on the new "soft despotism"[21]— both economic liberties and religious liberties are day by day tied down tight by Lilliputian threads. By attending mostly to man's material needs, and neglecting the needs of the free, creative, and responsible spirit, the new tyranny bases itself on a false anthropology, on a mere materialism imposed in the name of humanitarianism. This false humanitarianism makes a mockery of a true humanism.

At the heart of a true humanism lie coiled a liberty of spirit, conscience, responsibility, and ceaseless creativity. The new soft despotism reduces human beings to their merely animal capacities. It does not so much punish the creative as enervate them. It does not so much physically imprison the imaginative and the active, as suffocate them. The new soft despotism, like an invisible gas, slowly chokes all the spiritual energies of vital, energetic human persons, as if to reduce us to contented animals, to domesticate us, to render us dependent, quite tamed, and passive—munching contentedly in our stalls.

True human happiness lies in achievement, in creativity, in the spirited overcoming of obstacles and impediments. All this the new soft despotism would render impossible. A free economy, by contrast, blows out the sails of aspiration and achievement.

---

[21] Alexis de Tocqueville, *Democracy in America*, Vol. 2 (1840), bk. 4, chap. 6.

7

Why Religious Liberty Cannot Prosper without Economic Liberty

Jay W. Richards

In recent years, religious freedom in the United States has been treated by its defenders as a special form of freedom distinct from, say, political or economic freedom. This is not a viable long-term strategy for protecting religious freedom. Both economic and religious freedom tend to exist together in the same societies; they are both based on the same principles; they tend to reinforce each other; and over the long haul, they arguably stand or fall together. As a result, when Catholics and other Christians surrender economic freedom, they unwittingly surrender their religious freedom as well. The debate over the "HHS mandate," which violates the religious freedom of groups who supported the health care legislation of which it is a part, illustrates what happens when we fail to defend both economic and religious freedom.

To see this clearly, we must first unpack the idea of religious freedom itself.

The Implicit Basis for Religious Liberty

Our most important ideas are often the ones we take for granted; the unstated premises that inform as if by an invisible hand our conscious thoughts and deliberate actions. Because of the way religious freedom has developed and has been purified by history, it is easy for Americans to dwell blissfully in the branches of the tree of liberty and forget entirely the roots that anchor the tree to the ground.

We take it for granted that in matters of religious faith people should not be coerced. We assume that religious and political institutions should be separate. Indeed, most Americans think that true religious faith requires the exercise of freedom. We assume that that which is compelled is not true faith but mere pretense.

Few of us can articulate the original source for these convictions. I suspect this is because the theological premise that justifies it has become buried out of sight in the moral intuitions of even those who reject it. Thomas Jefferson summarized the premise as well as any when he wrote in the Declaration of Independence that we are endowed by our Creator with certain "unalienable rights," such as "life, liberty and the pursuit of happiness." If human beings have such rights by virtue of our divine origin, if we are the kind of creatures that ought to be accorded respect and given wide jurisdiction over the sorts of beliefs we affirm, then it follows that in certain matters, including but not limited to religion, no one should be coerced.

The American founder George Mason made the point lucidly in his draft of the Virginia Declaration of Rights (1776), a document that later became the model for the United States Bill of Rights:

> **Section 16.** That religion, or the duty which we owe to our Creator, and the manner of discharging it, can be directed only by reason and conviction, not by force or violence; and therefore all men are equally entitled to the free exercise of religion, according to the dictates of conscience; and that it is the mutual duty of all to practice Christian forbearance, love, and charity toward each other.[1]

Note that religious freedom here is not justified by relativism—the favorite but faulty argument of sophomores—but by reference to religion, by which Mason means the duty that each of us owes to God. The basis for religious liberty is itself religious.

George Mason, Thomas Jefferson, James Madison, and other American founders did not think they were invoking a parochial custom that they picked up from their European heritage. They claimed, rather, that these rights were universal, and that if one understood the truth about man, then one would simply see by reason that such rights obtained. They even went so far as to claim that the rights to life and liberty were self-evident.

---

[1] See the text of the Virginia Declaration of Rights at the National Archives website at http://www.archives.gov/exhibits/charters/virginia_declaration_of_rights.html.

Besides this commitment to the universal rights of man, the American founders were acutely aware of past religious conflicts, not just in far-away England but in the early American colonies as well. Although the founders were theologically diverse, they all believed that the existence of both a Creator and the moral law could be known by reason and should inform our legal and political lives. At the same time, they thought questions concerning the trinity, the proper form of baptism, church government, and the like were sectarian rather than strictly public concerns.

These dual convictions led them to a position perplexing both to modern secularists and to those who assume the founders meant to establish a Christian republic. The founders affirmed the public expression of religious faith and its importance to public morality while refusing to establish a national religion. Instead, they opted for widespread religious liberty, which meant that citizens could bring their religious convictions into the public square.

The First Amendment to the US Constitution captures their balanced approach: "Congress shall make no law respecting an establishment of religion, nor prohibiting the free exercise thereof." A just and limited state must recognize domains and institutions outside its jurisdiction. Such "prepolitical realities" include, most prominently, the right of every human being to "life, liberty and the pursuit of happiness." The right to liberty, in turn, implies a right to free speech, to freedom of association, and to freedom of religion.

This arrangement, they thought, would also prevent power from becoming concentrated in any single institution. The federal government would have three divided branches and a strictly defined jurisdiction, and would be limited by the states, by the rights of individuals, and by religious and other associations.

Separate religious institutions would, in turn, hold each other in check at the national level (at the time of the founding, the states did have established religions). Anyone who wanted Presbyterianism established would meet the resistance of Catholics. Anyone trying to establish Episcopalianism would have to deal with the Baptists. So, according to James Madison, for religious campaigns to succeed in American constitutional society, they would have to be based on "principles ... of justice and the common good."[2] These

---

[2] This is from *Federalist* 51, quoted in John West, *The Politics of Revelation and Reason* (Lawrence: University Press of Kansas, 1996), 213.

would usually involve individual Christians, not churches, forming voluntary groups to support causes consistent with natural law.[3]

Such clarity on the limits of government, the rights of conscience, and the free exercise of religion was a long time coming. It would have made little sense to Europeans in the year 1400, and it still makes little sense to hundreds of millions of people, many of them Muslim. Still, these ideas were seeds that grew in Judeo-Christian soil, and would have been unlikely to prosper in other fields. The moral intuitions of most Americans have been fed with the fruit grown from those earlier seeds, even if many have now forgotten it.

Dignitatis Humanae

The clearest expression of religious freedom for Catholics, and perhaps for Christianity in general, is found in the declaration *Dignitatis Humanae*, promulgated by Pope Paul VI on December 7, 1965. It emerged from the deliberations of the Second Vatican Council and is especially illuminating when read in light of the magisterial Vatican II Constitution on the Church in the Modern World, *Gaudem et Spes*.

Dignitatis makes clear that religious freedom is much broader than a mere "freedom to worship" or "freedom to hold religious beliefs." Again, it is grounded not in relativism but in a universal moral truth: the dignity of the human person. As free and rational creatures made in the image of God, persons should not be forced to violate their consciences in seeking to obey the moral law. Moreover, because God wants man to love him and to come to faith freely, man ought not, indeed, cannot be forced in these matters.

Because man is by nature a social creature, we also have a right to freedom of association. Religious communities by rights have the freedom to govern themselves within the confines of the natural law. Parents have the right and duty to educate their children in their faith. If people of a common religious outlook cannot gather together in communities, then they do not enjoy religious freedom but mere freedom to hold private religious beliefs.

Although *Dignitatis* does not speak of "limited government" in just those words, it is everywhere implied. Jesus' command to render to Caesar

---

[3] There is a difference between an official church, with official responsibilities, getting involved in the nitty-gritty of politics, and individual Christians doing so. You may have responsibilities as a citizen with economic expertise that your pastor, priest, or church would not have. See Michael Gerson and Peter Wehner, *City of Man: Religion and Politics in a New Era* (Chicago: Moody Publishers, 2010), 35–36.

what is Caesar's and to God what is God's, entails that the state has a limited jurisdiction. Then we have the example of Jesus himself, who never demanded us to compel unbelievers, but instead commanded us, "Go and make disciples of all nations." Faithful disciples come by way of persuasion and conviction, not sword and lash.

This is a very brief historical sketch of the American and Catholic idea of religious freedom. For our purposes, we can say that there is a *rough* agreement between the American founders' vision of religious freedom and the defense of that freedom in *Dignitatis Humanae*.

THE CORRELATION BETWEEN ECONOMIC AND RELIGIOUS FREEDOM

Religious freedom is not and should not be separated from economic freedom. In truth, these two types of freedom are intimately related and are separated at great peril, at least in the long run.

By economic freedom, I refer to the social condition in which individuals, families, and associations enjoy the rule of law, respect for their rights, limited government, a vibrant civil society outside the jurisdiction of the state, well-delineated rights to private property and contracts, and broad discretion on economic matters. If it is easy to start a business; to seek employment; to hire employees without invasive dictates from political authorities, private cartels, or organized crime; to negotiate salary, benefits, and responsibilities; to have fair contracts enforced; and the like, then a society enjoys some measure of economic freedom.

The Index of Economic Freedom,[4] published annually by the Heritage Foundation, compares the nations of the world with respect to economic freedom. In the 2015 index, Hong Kong is treated as a separate country and takes the top spot; followed by another city-state, Singapore; and then New Zealand, Australia, Switzerland, and Canada. For years, the United States was in the top ten, but in 2014, it dropped to twelve and remained in that spot in 2015.

At the bottom of the index (171–78), we find Iran, Turkmenistan, Equatorial Guinea, Eritrea, Zimbabwe, Venezuela, Cuba, and North Korea.

---

[4] See the current Index of Economic Freedom at http://www.heritage.org/index/.

The map that accompanies the index shows the mostly free countries in green, and the least free countries in red.⁵ The correlation between prosperity and freedom is obvious: the more economically free societies are uniformly prosperous and desirable to immigrants; the least economically free countries are precisely the opposite. Hong Kong is at the top. Stalinist North Korea is at the bottom. It is hard to miss the point.

The index focuses on economic rather than religious freedom. However there are other surveys of religious freedom, including an annual study by Pew and the annual reports by the US State Department.⁶ I am unaware of a rigorous study tying religious and economic freedom together, but a preliminary comparison suggests that, with a few exceptions, such as Singapore, economic and religious freedom correlate at the extremes. The State Department report highlights several violators of religious freedom, such as North Korea, Turkmenistan, and Iran, which rank at the very bottom of the economic freedom index. Similarly, laying the map of the Index of Economic Freedom over the Pew Forum map on religious freedom reveals a correlation at the extremes.⁷ That is, the most economically free regions tend also to be the regions with the most religious freedom. The least economically free tend to be the least free religiously.

The correlation is not perfect: There is a lot of scatter in the middle range, suggesting that it is possible, at least temporarily, for a nation to enjoy more economic than religious freedom, or vice versa. But the tight correlation at the extremes suggests that the two freedoms hang together. This is simply an empirical correlation and by itself does not establish a causal relation, but surely it is suggestive. To get a sense of how these two freedoms might be related, we have to dig deeper.

---

⁵ See also http://www.heritage.org/index/heatmap.

⁶ See, for instance, the Pew Forum's 2015 comparison of countries' freedom of religion at http://www.pewforum.org/2015/02/26/regions-and-countries/; "International Religious Freedom Report for 2013," issued by the State Department's Bureau of Democracy, Human Rights and Labor, at http://www.state.gov/j/drl/rls/irf/religiousfreedom/index.htm#wrapper.

⁷ The Pew Forum map published in 2015 (but indicating the scores for December 2013) available at http://www.pewforum.org/2015/02/26/religious-hostilities/restrictions2015-graphics_grimap640px/.

Economic and Religious Liberty Have the Same Foundation

As it happens, the philosophical basis for religious freedom rests on the same foundation as the case for economic freedom: individual rights, freedom of association and the family, and the presence of a government with limited jurisdiction.

Take first the intrinsic rights and dignity of the individual. Virtually all champions of economic liberty argue that human beings should enjoy certain rights and freedoms simply by virtue of being human. We find this in thinkers as diverse as Edmund Burke; Ludwig von Mises; F. A. Hayek; Thomas Sowell; Michael Novak; and even in her own eccentric way, Ayn Rand. With the exception of Novak, the idea tends to be treated simply as a premise: Individuals ought not to be unduly coerced unless they are directly violating the rights of others. There should be a wide space in which the individual should be free to act according the dictates of his conscience. Since Rand is the most extreme example—and by stereotype, least likely to be committed to the intrinsic dignity of human beings—I will quote her: "Man—every man—is an end in himself, not the means to the ends of others."[8]

From this premise follows a conclusion: Strong coercion over human beings should be limited primarily to cases in which one individual or group violates the intrinsic rights of another individual or group. Therefore, the state can rightly punish John if he has stolen twelve of Peter's sheep. If Peter is John's employee, and Peter and John have freely agreed to a specific payment for specific work, Peter should not be able to use the coercive power of the state to force John to pay him more, and John should not be able to coerce Peter into accepting less. John should not be able to compel Peter to remain his employee. If Peter believes he is not receiving fair payment from John for his labor, then he should be free to quit working for John and to work for James instead.

Freedom of association, the second foundation for religious freedom identified in *Dignitatis*, is also relevant. Employers should enjoy freedom in whom they choose to employ, as long as they do not violate the rights of others. At the same time, employees should enjoy freedom in their choices of employers within the same limits.

---

[8] Ayn Rand, *The Objectivist Newsletter* (August 1962): 35; as quoted in *The Ayn Rand Lexicon*, ed. Harry Binswanger, *The Ayn Rand Library*, vol. 4 (New York: Meridian, 1986), 343.

Though less obvious, the family's right of self-determination is also involved here. If I am free to raise and educate my children according to my religious convictions, then surely I should be free, *a fortiori*, to move with my family in search of employment, to start a business that involves my family (within limits), to provide for my family, and so forth.

Finally, economic freedom just as much as religious freedom requires limited government: a "government limited by laws." The government helps create and maintain the public space (along with other institutions of civil society) in which free economic decisions can be made. Economic freedom exists on a spectrum between anarchy at one extreme and statism on the other. A society in which the strong are "free" to prey on and enslave the weak is not economically free. Neither is a society free when all economic decisions are made by political fiat.

THE JUDEO-CHRISTIAN ORIGINS OF FREE INSTITUTIONS

Although it is still conventional wisdom in some circles to credit the late Enlightenment for the emergence of free institutions, careful historians have come to understand that the deep roots of these ideas are anchored, at least in part, in the Judeo-Christian tradition.

The first person to argue that Christian theology played a role in the emergence of economically free societies was Max Weber in *The Protestant Ethic and the Spirit of Capitalism* (1904–1905). The book was hugely influential and has given the English-speaking world the term *Protestant work ethic*. The details of Weber's thesis are problematic. Weber had an eccentric definition of puritanism and misread some historical details about the emergence of the economic ideas and institutions of medieval Europe. Still, he gets credit for arguing that theology can have a decisive effect on culture and economics at a time when such a thesis was quite controversial.

Much more recently, in 2005, sociologist Rodney Stark advanced the case for a broader Christian or Judeo-Christian origin for economic freedom in *The Victory of Reason*.[9] He credits belief in a rational God and in a rational and predictable universe, as well as commitments to reason, private property, the dignity of man as both a material and a spiritual being, the dignity of work, optimism but not utopianism, and limited government and the institutions of civil society. He even gives some credit to the long

---

[9] Rodney Stark, *The Victory of Reason* (New York: Random House, 2005).

and often obscure debate over the nature of usury and money lending. His conclusion: It is no coincidence that the institutions and ideas of economic freedom emerged in the Christian West rather than elsewhere. It is ironic that as these ideas have spread to the rest of the world, they have fallen into disfavor in the West.

For our purposes, the point is simply this: Religious and economic (as well as political) freedom emerged from the same complex mix of historical causes, suggesting once again that they are not easily separated.

The Feedback Between Religious and Economic Freedom

Because the economic and religious realms involve man as an individual, as a member of a family, and as a member of society, it is unrealistic to imagine that we can cordon off our religious liberty from our economic liberty.

Establishing this would require far more detail than I can offer here, but I would like to suggest, as a hypothesis, that there is a positive causal feedback between the two, which would explain the evidence we have already discussed. That is, an environment in which economic liberty is enjoyed is one in which religious liberty is likely to be enjoyed and vice versa. It is a virtuous circle. Similarly, in environments where our economic liberty is restrained, either by the state or by general lawlessness, our religious liberty is likely to suffer as well. This is a vicious circle.

If that is the case, then, if we wish to preserve religious liberty, what we need are robust defenses of *both* economic and religious liberty, framed in a way that makes it clear that these two liberties, these two freedoms, are mutually reinforcing and indivisible.

It does not follow that priests, bishops, and cardinals must all have graduate degrees in economics in order to defend religious freedom. Rather, they—we—all need to learn to practice the "art of economics."

Learning the Art of Economics

In his justly famous book *Economics in One Lesson*,[10] Henry Hazlitt describes the art (rather than the science) of economics thus: "The art of economics

---

[10] Originally published in 1946 by Harper and Bros., it is now available online by the Ludwig von Mises Institute, at http://mises.org/sites/default/files/Economics%20

consists in looking not merely at the immediate but at the longer effects of any act or policy; it consists in tracing the consequences of that policy not merely for one group but for all groups."

Hazlitt is describing an intellectual virtue that applies in every domain involving choices and actions, not just economics: actions and policies have consequences, and we bear some responsibility for policies and actions that have bad though unintended consequences if we could reasonably have anticipated those consequences. Fortunately, many economic and political policies have been tested over the last several centuries; we are not exactly flying in the dark. If a politician proposes stiff price controls on commodities in high demand or insists on raising the federal minimum wage to $100 an hour, we can predict with certainty what will happen.

Unfortunately, politicians are often rewarded for their stated intentions rather than the long-term consequences of their policies. As a result, democratic societies may be doomed always to have politicians who support destructive but politically useful policies. Still, pastors, priests, and religious Americans outside politics have a strong incentive to consider the consequences for religious freedom of policies that reduce economic freedom. Indeed it should have been obvious that the two health care reform acts passed in 2010, the Patient Protection and Affordable Care Act (PPACA) and the Health Care and Education Reconciliation Act (now collectively and commonly referred to as Obamacare), would lead, inevitably, to showdowns over religious freedom.

What Happens When We Do not Learn the Art of Economics: The Affordable Care Act and the HHS Mandate

For decades, the American health care market has suffered from what economists call the "third-party payer problem,"[11] which creates space between the provider and recipient of health care services. The recipients often have little to no knowledge or control over the prices of services. This prevents customers (patients in this case) from weighing the financial

---

in%20One%20Lesson_2.pdf.

[11] Maureen J. Buff and Timothy D. Terrell, "The Role of Third-Party Payers in Medical Cost Increases," *Journal of American Physicians and Surgeons* 19 (Summer 2014) at http://www.jpands.org/vol19no3/buff.pdf.

costs and benefits of services as they do in other markets. The effect is an increase in costs for the service.

The third-party payer problem started modestly during World War II, when wage controls led employers to seek other, nonwage forms of compensation for employees, such as health insurance, which were not subject to wage controls. Such compensation grew over time to include payment for ordinary services well outside of unexpected catastrophic events—the normal purpose for insurance. This "insurance" became a way of sheltering income from taxation by prepaying for routine medical services ahead of time. It is as if tax law encouraged us to purchase auto insurance that not only protected us from the rare collision but also paid for gas, car washes, tires, and oil changes, allowing us to access these services at will without considering the cost. We would not bother to look for bargains when we purchased gas and had our car serviced, and we would probably get far more car washes and tire replacements than if we experienced the costs at each point of service.

The third-party payer problem is why few of us know what the actual price of a doctor's visit or medical procedure is. Furthermore it is the primary reason that health care costs have gone up since the 1970s at over twice the rate of inflation.[12] (This issue does not exist in elective medical services, such as LASIK surgery and cosmetic surgery, where there is no third-party payer.)

This problem is not that complicated—I just summarized it in three paragraphs. It simply requires thinking about the way prices transmit information in a normal market setting. When prices accurately transmit to customers the underlying cost and demand for a good or service, then providers compete to offer the best service they can for the lowest price. Customers in turn shop around for precisely that.

Without a well-functioning market mechanism, third-party payers such as HMOs do what they can to control prices by negotiating fees with providers and restricting services to customers (often in the form of tedious procedural hurdles). When regulations prohibit or limit such defensive actions, the price of services goes up and is passed on to the employer who provides the insurance, and that may be passed on to the employee in the form of fees,

---

[12] Buff and Terrell, "The Role of Third-Party Payers in Medical Cost Increases," http://www.jpands.org/vol19no3/buff.pdf.

deductibles, and the like. Because there is no such thing as a free lunch, the rising costs have to be borne somewhere by someone.

In brief, the long-term effect of such a system is inefficiency, ever-increasing prices, and large numbers of people outside the system who cannot afford to purchase medical care out of pocket.

The two main problems that motivated health care reform were: (1) Americans paid more for their health care than most other developed countries, and (2) millions of people lacked health insurance altogether. In response to such problems, many well-meaning religious organizations, including the US Conference of Catholic Bishops, endorsed "health care reform," which by 2010 became *de facto* support for the Affordable Care Act (ACA) and the reconciliation act that accompanied it. There were concerns that some provisions of the ACA might infringe on religious freedom, but the general hope by Catholic bishops and others was that religious exemptions would prevent the rare cases of conflict, such as when Catholic hospitals or colleges might be compelled, without an exemption, to provide contraception or abortifacient drugs in their insurance plans.

The so-called HHS mandate—the rule from the Department of Health and Human Services that did not provide such an exemption—thus came as a shock because it meant that religious providers would be forced to pay for services they deemed to be morally objectionable. The result has been high profile cases involving both private corporations, such as Hobby Lobby, and religious organizations, such as Little Sisters for the Poor.[13] Still, the HHS mandate has been treated as if it were an anomaly, as if the ACA would not otherwise have infringed on the religious beliefs of Americans. This belief is probably misguided.

The medical sector in 2010 made up about 16 percent of the US economy. Insofar as the ACA surrendered economic freedom by shifting decisions in health care even farther away from the patients and providers and toward federal agencies, religious leaders should have expected that the ACA would inevitably infringe on religious freedom as well.

The sheer size of the legislation should have been a warning. During the debate over the Affordable Care Act, Republican opponents printed out the entire legislation, many hundreds of pages, to illustrate its sheer, unreadable size. (In contrast, the 1913 Federal Reserve Act was less than 40

---

[13] See the numerous news releases and responses to events related to the HHS mandate by the US Conference of Catholic Bishops at http://www.usccb.org/issues-and-action/religious-liberty/hhs-mandate/hhs-mandate-articles-and-news-releases.cfm.

pages long and contained fewer than 15,000 words.) All this made for great political theater, but critics pointed out that the number of pages depended on margins, font size, and the like.

Therefore, consider instead the number of words involved. The final health care legislation came to 381,517 words—about three-fifths of the length of *The Lord of the Rings* by J. R. R. Tolkien. That is pretty long, but it would have been possible for a legislator to read the entire legislation—though it is doubtful that anyone did.

Still, this is a drop in the bucket because legislation empowers regulatory agencies to write rules. This is the only way a law can be applied to thousands and thousands of concrete situations. As of October 2014, *11,588,500* words of regulations have been written as a result of the Affordable Care Act. Every word regulates a choice, action, or interaction among patients, hospitals, doctors, other health care providers, insurance companies, medical technology companies, and regulators themselves. It is absurd, in an era when abortion, abortifacient drugs, gender reassignment surgery, embryonic stem cell research, and the like are legally defined as health care, to imagine that such comprehensive interventions in the health care market would *not* lead to myriad conflicts with the religious freedom of health care and insurance providers.

Unfortunately, during the debates, many Catholic organizations publicly supported "comprehensive health care reform." Again, in the context of the debate, this was a *de facto* endorsement of the ACA, and provided it with essential moral cover in the pitched political battle.

Had Church spokesmen understood why health care costs were far higher than they ought to have been—primarily because of the third-party payer problem and malpractice insurance—they would have understood that the reform bill on offer had little prospect of lowering costs. In fact, the Affordable Care Act made the third-party payer problem far *worse* rather than better, and competent analysts explained this during the debate. The only way to keep costs down now, under the current system, will be either active or passive rationing of health services.

Now Catholic and other organizations are engaged in federal court battles to protect themselves from the ACA. Currently, the legal disputes involve the HHS mandate. The Catholic Church and many other Christians believe abortion is an intrinsic evil and thus object to regulations that compel them to provide insurance for such services. If they are victorious in court, some religious organizations and private companies with religious objections may be exempt from provisions that would compel them to engage in intrinsic moral evil. But thousands of companies and employers, who may not have such religious objections, will continue to be compelled to engage in these same moral evils. Legislation with such an outcome should never have enjoyed the aid and succor of Catholic leaders.

If the bishops and other religious leaders had anticipated these consequences, they could have helped stop bad legislation, headed off violations of religious freedom, and prevented the ongoing commission of intrinsic evils being paid for with tax dollars. The best we can do now is to treat the incident as a cautionary tale, which, if we remember it, might help us avoid similar mistakes in the future.

Part 3

CHRISTIANITY AND THE FOUNDATIONS OF A FREE SOCIETY: RELIGIOUS, POLITICAL, AND ECONOMIC FREEDOM

8

God, Reason, and Our Civilization Crisis

Samuel Gregg

Introduction

The subject of our reflections is Christianity's contribution to the growth of freedom and free societies, and more specifically to political, religious, and economic liberty. This subject needs more attention, not least because it is arguable that many people have become preoccupied, even fixated, in recent years with a different subject: equality. They have in mind not so much the idea of the equality of dignity first clearly expressed in the Hebrew Scriptures through the concept of all men being made as *imago Dei*, but, rather, equality in the sense of sameness of result, especially equal economic outcomes. In some instances, it has become difficult to distinguish particular Christian contributions to discussions about economic inequality from those of secular-minded people whose guiding principles seem far more rooted in the thought of Jean-Jacques Rousseau and what I have called "sentimental humanitarianism," rather than right reason and natural law.

This in turn points to a more general issue about freedom, the institutions of liberty, and Christianity. One of the ways in which Christianity has contributed to the growth of freedom is through its critical, if not unique, role in promoting natural law as the foundation for key principles and institutions that are central for free societies. Here I will try to illustrate why I think this is the case and why any loss of Christian attention to natural law can only have very negative implications for freedom. The place I would like to begin my reflections is with how we understand the nature of God and the significance of this for maintaining a *culture* of freedom.

Logos or sola Voluntas?

The word *culture* is derived from the Latin *cultus*. This broadly means "religious customs" or "rites." This illustrates that religion, in the sense of views about the Divine, is truly at the heart of any culture.

A particular religion's concept of God thus cannot help but influence the cultures in which that faith prevails. The ancient world, for instance, generally lacked the biblical notion of God as the Creator. Consequently, it did not view humans as "cocreators" working to unfold an unfinished creation in human history. This is one reason why the Greeks and Romans, unlike the Jews, viewed manual work and commerce as the responsibility of slaves, women, and other noncitizens.

Especially important, however, is the way that a religion's understanding of God impacts its appreciation of man's capacity for reason. This theme was central to Benedict XVI's discussion of the relationship between violence and religion in his 2006 Regensburg address.[1] If a religion does *not* regard God at some level as *Logos*—divine reason—rather than just an unmediated raw will, then that faith's capacity to dispute the reasonableness of those who, for instance, decapitate Christian hostages, burn prisoners-of-war to death, gun down cartoonists, slaughter Jews shopping in kosher-markets, and then claim religious warrants for doing so, is, at best, questionable.

In *Man and the State* (1951), the philosopher Jacques Maritain argued that it is necessary, on a political level, for all faiths and philosophies to agree that "violence is irrational." The focus, however, should not, he said, be on *why* any particular religion or philosophy might believe this to be the case. Yet Maritain himself conceded that sooner or later different religions and philosophies needed to address the issue of violence and religion at the level of theory if any agreement not to use violence was to hold politically.

Most contemporary discussion of these matters has focused, with good reason, on the connection between Islam's view of God and Islamic violence. Less attention, however, has been paid to the way in which the West's own loss of a sense of God as *Logos* helps explain why much of the West seems

---

[1] Pope Benedict XVI, "Faith, Reason, and the University: Memories and Reflections" (lecture, University of Regensburg, 12 September 2006). http://w2.vatican.va/content/benedict-xvi/en/speeches/2006/september/documents/hf_ben-xvi_spe_20060912_university-regensburg.html.

to be living in what the American natural-law philosopher, Robert George, aptly describes as "an Age of Feelings." Violence is not, after all, the only way in which profound irrationality can be expressed.

LOVE AND REASON, SENTIMENTALITY AND UNREASON

The two faiths at the core of Western culture—Judaism and Christianity—have long held that man is the *imago Dei*. It is worth asking, however, what happens to the way the West understands man's specific qualities as *imago* if the *Deus* becomes conceptualized primarily as a bundle of emotions and empathy instincts.

To different degrees and in varying ways, Judaism and Christianity express understandings of the Divine that accord significant places to love. When the God who reveals himself to Moses names himself as "I-AM," this underscores that the God of Abraham, Isaac, and Jacob is not a fable (i.e., an account of the world that does not conform to reality). Instead, Yahweh's very *be-ing* can be apprehended, albeit in limited ways, by man through the light of his *reason*. Appreciation of this insight may help account for why the Jews understood certain things far more clearly and earlier than did the Greeks. As the contemporary natural-law philosopher, John Finnis, pointed out in his 2014 Anscombe Memorial Lecture:

> The Jewish people and their true prophets *in fact* reached a settled and superior understanding of the universe's origins, and of its natural intelligibility, centuries earlier than the Greeks and their philosophers reached their own standard and in substance ... inferior understanding."[2]

Christianity is very explicit about the fact that *caritas* surpasses knowledge. However, Christianity's God of love does not cease to be *Logos*. The use of the expression "the Word" at the beginning of John's gospel reminded its heavily Gentile audiences that this gospel was a communication of divine reason. Only created beings graced with natural reason can be receptive to such a deity. Likewise, Saint Paul's reference in his *Letter to the Romans* to the law inscribed on all people's hearts led many of the earliest Christian thinkers, such as Theophilius of Antioch and Irenaeus, to immediately draw links between the Decalogue given to Israel by I-AM—a Decalogue

---

[2] John Finnis, "Body and Soul: On Anscombe's 'Royal Road' to True Belief" (lecture, The 5thAnscombe Memorial Lecture, St. John's College, Oxford, October 14, 2014). It can be viewed at https://www.youtube.com/watch?v=zUmd_3SEGis.

convincingly reaffirmed by Christ and Paul, especially the negative commandments inscribed on the second tablet—and the idea of natural law written into man's very reason itself.

A World without Logos

Once, however, *Logos* as a prominent dimension of God's nature starts fading from Western culture's horizons, what is left? There appear to be three possibilities.

One is "God-as-Will," but untethered to reason. This is a God who acts arbitrarily—one we must simply obey. Freedom is thus found in unquestioning submission, no matter how irrational the divine command. Another is "God-as-Love" but without reasonableness. This is a God who, like an irresponsible parent, simply affirms his child's choices, no matter how foolish or evil such decisions might be. A third possibility is "God-beyond-Reason." This produces a narrowed understanding of human reason itself: one that confines our rationality to the verifiable scientific method and thereby declines to permit it to ponder the bigger questions opened by the intriguing possibility that divine reason exists.

If any of these concepts of God prevail in a culture, we can hardly be surprised that attempts to answer *why* we make particular choices—moral, political, legal, and economic—or *why* we think freedom is important become reduced to strongly felt emotions, utilitarian calculations, or, more recently, what the philosopher Tyler Burge calls "neurobabble."[3] Instead of seeking rational resolutions to problems, we increasingly defer to reigning majority opinion, panels of experts, the posturing of populist politicians, consequentialist rationalizations devised to legitimize all sorts of evil, or some type of force—whether expressed though democratically elected temporary majorities or outright coercion.

Herein lies my central point: Notions of natural law and right reason become much harder to comprehend in these circumstances. After all, if the God who created man is an irrational entity, or just another sentimental humanitarian, why should we expect humans to be reasonable? Why should we expect people to make rational choices? Why should we care whether people are free or not free?

---

[3] Tyler Burge, "A Real Science of Mind," *New York Times*, December 19, 2010, http://opinionator.blogs.nytimes.com/2010/12/19/a-real-science-of-mind/?_r=1.

What makes humans different from animals—and opens up the very possibility of civilization in the first place—is our capacity for natural reason and free choice. These enable us to resist our baser predispositions, to know the good, and then to freely choose it. Yet, it is very challenging for a culture to sustain this specific vision of reason and free choice if it conceptualizes God as a cosmic will capable of contradicting himself, or as a celestial teddy bear whose prime responsibility is to cuddle us, or as a supreme watchmaker who allows us to discover the mechanics of how things work but does not regard us as worthy of knowing his deeper reasons for creating the world.

Today, the Islamic world is struggling with a particularly virulent God problem. For everyone else, this matters because, while we can protect ourselves to an extent against those who want us to submit to a thoroughly voluntaristic vision of a God who acts unreasonably, at some point the cessation of Muslim violence is going to require many Muslims to *change their minds* about God's nature.

Yet, anyone who cares about Western civilization should also remember that no matter how materially prosperous and technologically advanced we become or how much we celebrate concepts such as rule of law, the coherence of these achievements will be increasingly tenuous if our culture-forming institutions—ranging from families and universities to synagogues and churches—continue embracing sentimentalist concepts of God.

In that regard, I would submit, there is a real danger that the present emphasis on mercy in the Church could degenerate—in some cases it already has—into an understanding of love devoid of reason. This in turn, threatens the very coherence of a number of institutions that promote liberty.

One example concerns a key idea that is especially important for political and economic freedom. I am referring to the values, institutions, and protocols associated with what we call the rule of law.

In 2012, the financier George Soros and the head of one of the world's largest antipoverty NGOs, Fazle Hasan Abed, pointed out in the *Financial Times* that, despite the Great Recession, the number of people living in extreme poverty had fallen in every region of the world for the first time since record-keeping had begun.[4] That story—and many others concerning measurable decline in poverty and decline in economic inequality as more

---

[4] George Soros and Fazel Hasan Abed, "Rule of Law Can Rid the World of Poverty, *Financial Times*, September 26, 2012, http://www.ft.com/intl/cms/s/0/f78f8e0a-07cc-11e2-8354-00144feabdc0.html#axzz3ka8aoDZg.

people participate in global markets[5]—are often ignored today, including by many Christians. Why? One reason is that such developments do not fit populist narratives that rely on demonstrably false claims that global economic inequality is increasing.

Soros and Abed, however, then argued that the road out of poverty was fundamentally compromised by the absence of the rule of law in many developing countries. "Poverty," they claimed, "will only be defeated when the law works for everyone." If that is true, then countries such as China and India, which have taken hundreds of millions out of poverty in recent decades but that also rank relatively low on virtually every rule of law index, still face significant challenges.[6]

The wider background to this growing attentiveness to the rule of law's significance in reducing poverty is a realization that widening access to economic growth's benefits and maintaining prosperity have far less to do with wealth redistribution than with a country's institutional settings. More work, however, is needed to understand the ways in which *value* choices affect the type of institutions that emerge, how they function, and their impact on problems such as poverty.

Legal philosophers have long been divided about how much moral capital is invested in the idea of the rule of law. In the 1960s, for example, the Harvard legal philosopher Lon Fuller argued that the criteria he associated with the rule of law—such as that legal rules are prospective not retroactive, rules are promulgated and are clear and coherent, and rules are not impossible to comply with—reflected a type of inner morality and made it harder for tyrants to get their way.[7]

Fuller's position was criticized by Oxford's H. L. A. Hart. Hart claimed that such processes, as valuable as they are, had not significantly inhibited unjust regimes such as National Socialist Germany from pursuing diabolical

---

[5] Nicholas Eberstadt, "How the World Is Becoming More Equal," *Wall Street Journal*, August 26, 2014, http://www.wsj.com/articles/nicholas-eberstadt-how-the-world-is-becoming-more-equal-1409095792.

[6] See the Property Rights Charts and other data for these countries as presented by the Heritage Foundation's Index of Economic Freedom, http://www.Heritage.org/index/.

[7] Lon L. Fuller, *The Morality of Law*, rev. ed. (1965; repr., New Haven, CT: Yale University Press, 1977).

ends. Fuller's response was to insist that no tyranny had ever developed where rule of law was truly maintained.[8]

The fact that strong rule of law generally correlates with greater economic prosperity for all seems hard to deny. Such conditions are more conducive for attracting, for instance, foreign investment.

But here is my point: If the only moral grounding for the rule of law is its wealth-enhancing potential, it could theoretically be nullified by governments that insist that different arrangements would facilitate more rapid economic development. This is not as unlikely a scenario as some imagine. Many twentieth-century Communist regimes and Marxist legal philosophers derided rule of law as a "bourgeois device," designed to keep the proletariat in their place.[9] As an alternative, they proposed legal systems built on "the people's justice" or "socialist justice"—constructs that, in the name of seeking to create better economic conditions for those in need, legitimized inflicting vast systematic injustices on millions.

WHAT GROUNDS THE RULE OF LAW? FREEDOM AND REASON

What, then, might be deeper moral foundations for the rule of law that support but go beyond the benefits of economic growth? Two seem to be especially pertinent.

The Scottish founder of modern economics, Adam Smith, observed long ago that the economic well-being of "an industrious and frugal peasant" in eighteenth-century Western Europe was probably less than that of a "European prince" but would certainly exceed "that of many an African king, the absolute master of the lives and liberties of ten thousand naked savages."[10]

Smith is making a point about relative poverty, but it is not simply the material differences to which Smith is alluding. Smith's European peasant is not just better off than the African tyrant and his subjects because he is wealthier than they are. Smith's European peasant is also a free man,

---

[8] See Fuller, "A Reply to Critics," in *The Morality of Law*, chap. 5.

[9] See Martin Krygier, "Marxism and the Rule of Law: Reflections after the Fall of Communism," *Law & Social Inquiry* 15 (Autumn 1990): 633–63.

[10] Adam Smith, *An Inquiry into the Nature and Causes of the Wealth of Nations* (1776), vol. 1, bk. 1, sec. 11, http://www.econlib.org/library/Smith/smWN1.html.

thanks partly to the rule of law. Unlike those under the African king, the state cannot do whatever it likes to him. Rule of law is thus rooted in the liberty it provides each person through the substantive equality it accords everyone before the law.

A second principle on which rule of law is grounded becomes apparent when we realize that all of the conditions that constitute rule of law underscore a commitment to *nonarbitrariness*: in other words, that there are *reasonable* ways of acting. It is unreasonable, for instance, to pass laws with which no one can comply. In short, a moral good from which the rule of law derives its inner coherence is *reason* itself. It is the type of reason that allows us to say that this head of state is acting unjustly when she acts "extra-constitutionally" while that judge is acting reasonably when he recuses himself from a case in which he is seen to have a conflict of interest.

Economies and Laws Worthy of Man

Therefore, at the core of the rule of law's reliance on commitments to goods such as freedom and reason is another key revelation: we expect the law's internal workings to be underpinned by reason and to facilitate human freedom because we think there is something distinct about *all* human beings that makes them worthy (*dignus*) of such treatment. That should remind us *why* we want as many people as possible to escape the material poverty that attracts our sympathy.

It should not be merely because we do not want people to suffer. Although that is important, our commitment to fighting poverty should also reflect a conviction that human beings are free, possess reason, and are therefore capable of flourishing, including in the economy. In short, rule of law reflects a moral investment in legal systems that "fit" the truth that humans are rational and free people.

Therein lies a message for anyone who is concerned about poverty. If we want to be coherent when addressing poverty, rather than populists or sentimentalist do-gooders, our concerns cannot be rooted in emotivist, skeptical, or relativistic accounts of who human beings are. If people become subject to arbitrary rule or backbreaking material poverty, that should be seen as an infringement on their reason and their freedom and therefore a violation of their dignity. The very same dignity also provides direction to the ways in which we seek to realize conditions that provide some minimal economic certainty while preserving the space that people need to use their reason and freedom to flourish in the economy.

This should also turn anyone concerned about poverty away from focusing exclusively on redistribution and toward realizing that, as the economist Julian Simon put it, man is indeed man's greatest resource.[11] This is true not just economically but also in terms of man's unique capacity to *know* the basic moral goods on which our most effective poverty-reducing institutions rely for their very rationality.

To put it simply, poverty reduction is very difficult without rule of law. Rule of law is in turn very difficult to maintain over the long term without being grounded in natural law. Natural law in turn depends on an understanding that God is *Logos*: God is divine reason. It follows that sentimentalist concepts of God undermine the idea of natural law, which in turn undermines the idea of rule of law, which in turn undermines a society's capacity to promote freedom and reduce poverty. It turns out that God—especially our understanding of who he is—really matters.

If Catholics and other Christians are serious about all these things, it therefore seems that one way that they can contribute to the protection and revival of freedom—political freedom, religious freedom, and economic freedom—is to engage natural theology and natural law far more seriously. Because, if we are honest with ourselves, we should recognize that knowledge of basic precepts of natural law, the teaching of natural law, and the understanding of natural law have visibly withered in much of the Catholic Church since the 1960s.

On one level, this is puzzling. An important document of the Second Vatican Council, the *Declaration on Religious Liberty* (*Dignitatis Humanae*), is grounded very clearly on arguments based not on relativism, not on John Locke's notions of tolerance, not on classical or modern liberalism, but rather on natural law. According to *Dignitatis Humanae*, religious liberty is a right grounded in the truth—knowable by natural reason—that man is a truth-seeker, including the truth about God and the ultimate meaning of life, and that man needs the freedom to seek this truth, free from the threat of unreasonable coercion. The Council was also very clear that the limits of religious liberty and the state's specific responsibilities in regulating religious liberty are also derived from natural law.

---

[11] See Julian L. Simon, *The Ultimate Resource 2* (Princeton: Princeton University Press, 1996).

There are some exceptions to this widespread neglect of natural law in the Church today. In the Anglo-Saxon Catholic world, for example, natural-law thinking has undergone a profound revival over the past thirty years. This has added considerable focus, coherence, and clarity to the Church's engagement in the public square that is not so easy to detect, for instance, in whatever is left of continental Western European Catholicism.

Perhaps the pope who has most underscored this point is one who I am convinced will one day be a Doctor of the Church. In a series of addresses—Regensburg, Paris, London, Berlin—this great pope stressed again and again that the maintenance of freedom and free societies depends on broadening our concept of reason and "overcom[ing] the self-imposed limitation of reason to the empirically falsifiable." Pope Benedict pointed to theology as having a critical role to play—not merely as a historical discipline, and certainly not as a way of rationalizing the rampant sentimentalism that is currently damaging the Church and destroying the West from within. Rather, Benedict held, theology should contribute to saving reason and therefore freedom, "precisely as theology, as inquiry into the rationality of faith."[12]

Conclusion

If we care about freedom—whether it is political freedom, economic freedom, or religious freedom—we have to care about reason, and we have to care about the ultimate foundation of reason. "The West," Benedict once wrote, "has long been endangered by ... aversion to the questions that underlie its rationality."[13] To put it another way and in the words of the Anglican theologian Ian Markham: "You cannot assume a rationality and then argue that there is no foundation to that rationality. Either God and rationality go or God and rationality stay. Either Nietzsche or Aquinas, that is our choice."[14]

If freedom is to prevail, it is a choice we need to make as well.

---

[12] Pope Benedict XVI, "Faith, Reason, and the University: Memories and Reflections" (lecture, University of Regensburg, 12 September 2006). http://w2.vatican.va/content/benedict-xvi/en/speeches/2006/september/documents/hf_ben-xvi_spe_20060912_university-regensburg.html.

[13] Pope Benedict XVI, "Faith, Reason, and the University."

[14] Ian Markham, *Truth and the Reality of God: An Essay in Natural Theology* (Edinburgh, Scotland: T&T Clark, 1998), 115.

9

FAITH AND FREEDOM AND THE ESCAPE FROM POVERTY

Anielka Münkel Olson

Five years ago, I was part of a PovertyCure team that visited Argentina in search of stories that would help us to understand what communities need in order to be prosperous and what conditions the human person requires to utilize the potential that God has endowed each of us with. Here I would like to focus on three points that emerged from that search. The first is the current model of what has happened in the fight against poverty and what the ideas underlying these current strategies are. The second will be effectiveness—what we have learned especially with regard to initiatives that affirm the origin and the destiny of the human person. The third will be the Catholic tradition and what it brings to the table. I strongly believe that we need to be aware of the insights of our tradition on this topic because only then will we be able to defend ourselves and know what we are losing as we face so many attacks on the liberty and the dignity of the human person.

A central theme of Catholicism is the fight against poverty, as it is of Christianity more generally. Pope Francis has called us to avoid being part of what he calls "the globalization of indifference." As Christians, we are called to let ourselves be loved by God and to love others. If we are going to love others, then we cannot be indifferent to the pain that we see in those around us. Saint John Paul II said that the fight against poverty is one of the greatest moral challenges of our time.

The Contemporary Situation in Poverty Aid

Where are we today? It is clear that we have made great strides in the fight against poverty. If we look at the situation two hundred years ago, the per capita GDP of only a small handful of countries exceeded three thousand dollars, and the average life expectancy was forty years.[1] The reality for many parts of the world is different nowadays, but we are dealing with new challenges. One of the most important steps to take in the fight is to study and understand the change that took place over those two centuries. Once we take a closer look, we will learn that these changes are not the result of aid. These changes are not the result of a donation model. They are instead the result of allowing human beings to utilize the talents God has bestowed on them so as to provide for their own families in a globalized world.

The model of sending material things to people in need appears to be way too simple, yet it is the prevailing approach that international organizations, governments, and other development agencies follow. It is something that I also thought about as a little girl growing up in Nicaragua. I remember reflecting on poverty at a very young age, because I could tell that many of the children I saw in my town would have a different future than mine. I remember asking: Why was I born to this family when I could have very well been one of these other children? How could I bring about an end to this apparent injustice? The solution that I came up with entailed providing these children with everything they needed to be happy. Back then, my idea was to have a flying bicycle that would bring toys, food, and clothing to people around the world.

Although I can now laugh about the idea of a flying bike, I cannot laugh at the sad reality that this model still prevails at most organizations devoted to helping those suffering from the consequences of material poverty. When we think about alleviating poverty, the immediate response usually seems to be: what am I going to give to this person?

In our work with PovertyCure and through my own professional and educational journey, I have learned that aid models tend to foster dependency, and they can deform the culture of entire countries. People may come to think that the solution no longer depends on them; instead, they will wait for someone from abroad to come and change their situation. Considering the impact of this model at the local level, we have found

---

[1] Comparisons can be explored at Gapminder.org (see the Gapminder World tab).

that despite good intentions, donations sent to developing countries can have a negative effect in the local economy. We tend to forget that in those countries there are producers and there are entrepreneurs who are trying to earn their daily bread by providing a good or service. When we simply send something, such as food to Haiti or clothes to Africa, without regard to the consequences, we are posing a threat to the local businesspeople.

Another of the models that has been applied to development in the last sixty years is that of foreign aid, or government-to-government transfers. This model is complex but also inadequate to respond to the needs of local communities. For example, Haiti was self-sufficient in rice production until the 1980s, but over the years, the United States requested that they lower their tariffs on rice imports to 3 percent.[2] Then, highly subsidized US rice flooded the Haitian markets and destroyed the rice industry in that country. We had an opportunity to talk to rice farmers in Haiti, and they told us that instead of having the United States send them free rice, what they would like to do is produce and export their rice to the United States and other countries. In this simple comment, we can see the desire of the human heart to provide for one's family, to be responsible, and to use the talents one has received from God.

A third model that has received a great deal of attention is social entrepreneurship. Consider the One for One model of the company TOMS Shoes, currently the best-known example of this model. The goal here is not to criticize those who started this company but to show that this mind-set of trying to alleviate poverty by providing material goods to people pervades all levels. It was very interesting to hear the reaction of people in Haiti to this approach. After watching the video that explains this model, entrepreneur Daniel Jean-Louis told us: "No one in Haiti wants to be a beggar for life." No one will want to receive shoes for a lifetime. The premise of this model is that when we buy a product another person around the world will receive a copy of what we bought. Who would have thought that this could have negative consequences? Well, we need to think about the impact on the local economy and on the local businesses, but more importantly, about the impact of the ideas we are promoting with a culture of donations.

We are in front of an industry with many actors who share a common vision. Despite the good intentions of so many people, we have created a

---

[2] Josiane Georges, "Trade and the Disappearance of Haitian Rice," TED Case Studies No. 725, June 2004, http://www1.american.edu/TED/haitirice.htm.

poverty industry.[3] In the midst of this complex system, one of the delicate and problematic assumptions is a mistaken concept of the human person, and this has grave consequences. When we fail to understand that each person created by God has capacity, has a responsibility to use his talents, is a potential cocreator, is an innovator, and is not a mere consumer—then we start to see *people* as the problem.

The way we deal with the challenge of poverty, the way we look at the world, will change radically depending on our understanding of the human person. A few years ago the *Economist* brought to light the abuse of gendercide.[4] This is what is taking place in countries such as China, where the government has restricted the freedoms of families by imposing a one-child policy. As a result, parents are forced to choose between having a boy or a girl. In the vast majority of cases, they choose boys. Basically, there is a war against females. The *New York Times Magazine* also touched on this subject when it referred to a "daughter deficit," and most recently the documentary *It's a Girl!* has exposed the gravity of this issue.[5] In this film, we hear that in some countries those three words are like a death sentence. It is of utmost importance for us to realize the serious consequences of having a wrong concept of the human person. In China, there are currently forty million more men than women.[6] These are men who will not find someone to marry because of this deficit of women. The normal male to female ratio for a population is 105 men for 100 women; this is the way nature has kept a balance in our populations throughout history. In China, however, there are many rural areas with a ratio of 100 women for each 140 men.

As Christians who are concerned with applying our faith in the international arena, we are called to defend life and be a voice for those who cannot defend themselves. Unfortunately, many international development organizations view the human person as the problem, and this view is

---

[3] This topic is the focus of the award-winning documentary, *Poverty, Inc.*

[4] "Gendercide," *The Economist*, March 4, 2010, http://www.economist.com/node/15606229.

[5] Tina Rosenberg, "The Daughter Deficit," *New York Times Magazine*, August 19, 2009, http://www.nytimes.com/2009/08/23/magazine/23FOB-idealab-t.html?pagewanted=2&_r=0; see http://www.itsagirlmovie.com/.

[6] Nicholas Eberstadt, "The Global War Against Baby Girls," *The New Atlantis*, no. 33 (Fall 2011): 3–18, http://www.thenewatlantis.com/publications/the-global-war-against-baby-girls.

prevalent in widely accepted goals such as the United Nations Millennium Development Goals. These include abortion practices and population control mechanisms that set limits on populations and on the freedoms we have received from God.

What does our faith tell us? We are called to live *caritas*, but this love, as Benedict XVI said, has to be grounded on reason and truth, otherwise it will be mere sentimentalism.[7] As Christians, we have a big responsibility because if we truly understand what it means to live this love, we cannot continue our lives in the same way. To live the virtue of *caritas* means to desire the good of the other, and as we deal with the challenge of poverty, living this virtue means that we are going to put the other person's good before our own. We are going to try to see the situation through the eyes of the other and first think, if I was in that situation, how would I want to be treated? When I was in Haiti, I spoke to an entrepreneur and asked him: "If you didn't have a job and someone came to you and said, 'Don't worry, I will take care of your kids. I will bring them to this orphanage. They will still be your kids but I will provide for them'—how would you feel"? And he said, "I would never want that; who would?" However, currently there are many programs that promote that very model.

With PovertyCure we state that we are going to live this virtue of charity and that one of its critical elements is a correct understanding of the origin and destiny of the human person. In our logo, the human person appears at the center because this echoes the teachings of our Church. We have to understand that we are made in the image and likeness of God, with an eternal destiny. When we truly embrace this truth, our way of responding to the challenge of poverty will be transformed. Each person—even the beggars we see in the street, even those who seem not to have capacity—has received a mission from God.

What then is the way to help each person live his calling? In most cases, the answer will be *work*. The Gallup organization conducts a worldwide poll to try to understand what people want, and the most common answer to this question is a job.[8] Arthur Brooks has also conducted much research

---

[7] See Samuel Gregg, "God, Reason, and Our Civilization Crisis," chap. 8 above.

[8] Gallup Poll, "What Everyone in the World Wants: A Good Job," *Business Journal*, June 9, 2015, http://www.gallup.com/businessjournal/183527/everyone-world-wants-good-job.aspx.

about the notion of earned success and its correlation with happiness.[9] Based on these insights, it follows that if we want to have countries with happier people and people who fulfill their callings, then we have to allow them to use their talents in a job.

Entrepreneurship is critical for job creation, though it is foreign to the experience of many in Latin America. The dominant tradition in this part of the world is not free and competitive markets but oligarchic capitalism. Under this model, people find it very difficult to think of themselves as entrepreneurs when they grow up, and they end up not being part of a group that could potentially change the future of a country. Part of the solution is to develop ethical businesses led by people who will live the calling of honoring God in everything they do—in their work, in their family, in all aspects of their life. As those stories are shared, we will eventually start to change the perception that businesspeople take advantage of others.

The idea of getting ahead of others has been ingrained in our tradition since colonial times. In Nicaragua, our first folkloric piece, *El Güegüense*, is a clear example of this. The play showcases how the mestizos would make fun of the Spanish and try to take advantage of them as a way to get back at them. Our faith with its moral foundation is the key to break away from models that perpetuate endless cycles of corruption and lack of trust. Rafael Di Tella, an Argentinian professor at Harvard University, has studied corruption in Latin America. He concludes that corruption is indeed one of the reasons why capitalism does not triumph in this region.[10] Di Tella asserts that when citizens perceive corruption they will try to punish the business leaders who have benefited from an alliance with the government. This reaction explains the cycles of populism we have seen in our countries, as people feel dissatisfied by the high levels of cronyism in our governments.

In concrete terms, as we at PovertyCure think of entrepreneurship, we focus on microfinance and the role of small and medium enterprises (SMEs). Microfinance is one of the easiest models to understand and many people start there. Research from the Center of International Development at Harvard, however, shows that we need to pay more attention to SMEs.

---

[9] Arthur C. Brooks, *Gross National Happiness: Why Happiness Matters for America—and How We Can Get More of It* (New York: Basic Books, 2008).

[10] Rafael Di Tella and Robert MacCulloch, "Why Doesn't Capitalism Flow to Poor Countries?" *Brookings Papers on Economic Activity*, Spring 2009, http://www.brookings.edu/~/media/Projects/BPEA/Spring-2009/2009a_bpea_ditella.PDF.

These businesses employ more than 65 percent of people in the United States and European countries and also represent 95 percent of the total number of businesses in those same countries.

Among the people we visited in Haiti was an entrepreneur whose company makes solar panels. It employs men who come from a neighborhood that the United Nations has declared to be among the most dangerous place on earth. When we talked to these men and visited their families, we learned that they are like any other fathers wishing to provide for their children. We learned that this company often competes with the donations that are sent to Haiti, and, after the earthquake, it was almost put out of business because of those well-intended efforts.

FAITH AND THE PRINCIPLES OF A PROSPEROUS SOCIETY

What does our faith tradition bring to this discussion? This is a crucial question to address but unfortunately not very many educational programs delve into it. For me, this was a powerful discovery in my years at Acton. It was like the pieces of the puzzle all came together and I could finally understand what our communities needed in order to thrive. In God's plan, when he created man free, he provided a framework for human flourishing with institutions that would affirm our very nature. Religious freedom is a crucial element in this model, which can be outlined according to the following principles.

Private Property

This concept appears in the Old Testament as the simple truth that we cannot be generous with something that does not belong to us. There are many studies about the importance of private property. Peruvian economist Hernando de Soto has studied this topic extensively and explains that capitalism succeeded in the United States and Europe because these regions already had clear property titles and a stable rule of law. He estimates that the total value of the real estate held but not legally owned by the poor of the developing world and former communist nations is at least $9.3 trillion.[11] This means that the poor already have what they need to get out of poverty,

---

[11] Hernando de Soto, *The Mystery of Capital: Why Capitalism Triumphs in the West and Fails Everywhere Else* (New York: Basic Books, 2000).

but they lack the means of using that property as leverage to advance in the modern economy.

I have also mentioned the study conducted by Argentinian professors Rafael Di Tella and Ernesto Schradgosky about the impact of private property on a person's worldview. It was an honor for me to talk with them five years ago and learn about this natural experiment. It all started in 1981 when squatters invaded some parcels of land on the outskirts of Buenos Aires. As time went by, the government was able to obtain title for many of the settlers, but not for all. Thirty years later, the professors studied the two groups and concluded that those who had received title to their land shared many of the same values as middle-income people in Argentina. They trusted others more, they believed their future depended on themselves, they had higher education and better health, and they even had better kept homes.[12]

Private property has been addressed in several encyclicals, and in *Rerum Novarum* it appears as a key principle, which provides the space for families to develop and for parents to share their values.

Rule of Law

Studies show that there is a greater correlation between rule of law and development than there is between democracy and development. This is a challenge for us in Latin America and for many countries around the world. However, we know that institutions will be a reflection of the people who are part of them, and I believe that the way to address this issue is to focus on the formation and mind-set change of those people.

Freedom of Association

When we speak of free association, we go back in time to the beginning of universities, hospitals, and businesses. Each person possesses the right to associate with others for the purpose of pursuing a common good. In many places in the world today, this freedom is being restricted.

---

[12] Rafael Di Tella, Sebastian Galiani, and Ernesto Schargrodsky, "The Formation of Beliefs: Evidence from the Allocation of Land Titles to Squatters," *Quarterly Journal of Economics* 122 (February 2007): 209–41.

Freedom of Exchange

I mentioned the case of Haiti in our opening. We currently do not have free exchange but unfair trade policies on behalf of the United States and European countries, which continue subsidizing sectors of their economies while imposing tariffs on foreign goods.

Families, Communities, and Civil Society

If we look at our personal experience, we will note that, as Pope Francis has said, we learned the values that direct our lives in our families. Here the church has a very important role as well, and it is encouraging for us to see that many religious leaders share this special mission of helping and forming others in this path.

A Culture of Trust

At the foundation of this framework, we find a culture of trust. This element is a challenge for us because, given our tradition in Latin America, this culture of trust takes time to develop. Experts around the world show that it is an indispensable element for a country to be prosperous over time. If people cannot enter into a professional agreement or have relationships that are based on transparency, there can be no prosperity.

I would like to touch on culture because this is an area that gives us hope for the future. I realize that this is a delicate topic because it is not acceptable to say that a culture of trust is applicable to all societies and all cultures. However, our research indicates that we can change culture, and this culture is a foundation for all the other institutions we previously described. Michael Fairbanks, who has been an advisor for PovertyCure, has worked extensively on this topic and the idea of mental models. He states that by asking three questions, he can predict the future of a country. He can conclude that they are on the road to prosperity or that they will remain in poverty. The first question is: "Do you believe in competition?" The second one has to do with a fixation with the past or the future, and the third one has to do with complexity.

What does religious freedom have to do with this? We have mentioned several freedoms, and they are all interconnected. The term *religious freedom* was coined by Tertullian, one of the fathers of our Church, in the year 197 AD. In his *Apologeticum*, he stated:

> Look to it, whether this also may form part of the accusation of irreligion—to do away with freedom of religion, to forbid a man choice of deity, so that I may not worship whom I would, but am forced to worship whom I would not. No one, not even a man, will wish to receive reluctant worship.[13]

We ought to be proud that in our Church's tradition we find the foundation of so many ideas that are today being attacked.

Although the relationship between religious and economic freedom has not been studied extensively, the Religious Freedom Project of the Berkley Center for Religion, Peace, and World Affairs at Georgetown University has taken this topic as the focus of its research in the last few years. In one study, Professor Timothy Shah and Professer Anthony Gill concluded that there is a connection among religious liberty, economic liberty, and prosperity.[14] In contrast to other studies that tended to separate these two liberties, Shah and Gill highlight eight pathways that illustrate how religious freedom allows human beings to live up to their potential and achieve prosperity. One of these paths is the propagation of ideas. When a community has religious freedom, its members can live their own faith, and they will organize in ways that resemble those of an enterprise—for example, by providing training, by promoting a mission, and by furnishing resources to promote a message. They argue that, because many of the concepts and the virtues that a religious group wants its members to live by are applicable in a market economy, the propagation of religion can lead to economic prosperity. They also speak of immigration. When a country does not violate the principles of religious freedom, talented individuals from other countries will no doubt come and settle in that country and live their faith without restrictions. In their research, Shah and Gill also indicate that there is a relationship between a decrease in religious liberty and an increase in violence, as we are witnessing in some many regions of the world today.

---

[13] Tertullian, *Apologeticum*, as quoted in "Christianity and the Discovery of Religious Freedom" by Hartmut Leppin, *Rechtsgeschichte—Legal History Rg* 22 (2014): 62–78, http://dx.doi.org/10.12946/rg22/062-078.

[14] Timothy Shah and Anthony Gill, *Religious Freedom, Democratization, and Economic Development: A Survey of the Causal Pathways Linking Religious Freedom to Economic Freedom and Prosperity and Political Freedom and Democracy* (paper presented at the Annual Meeting of the Association for the Study of Religion, Economics, and Culture, Washington, DC, April 13, 2013).

Poverty is complex. We have looked at the current models, at what is effective, and at what insights our faith brings to the table. We are facing a clear attack to our liberty, but I think that something as simple as the fruits of the Holy Spirit can guide us in the right direction. They can indicate what we need to strive for. When we think of developing that culture of trust, we need to think of each person who is next to us, in our families and in our workplaces, because we have to give witness of our faith, based on reason and charity, to each person we encounter.

I would like to close with some remarks from St. John Paul II's address to the United Nations. He said,

> We must not be afraid of the future.... It is no accident that we are here. Each and every human person has been created in the "image and likeness" of the One who is the origin of all that is. We have within us the capacities for wisdom and virtue. With these gifts, and with the help of God's grace, we can build in the next century and the next millennium a civilization worthy of the human person, a true culture of freedom.[15]

---

[15] Pope John Paul II, (address to the Fiftieth General Assembly of the United Nations Organization, October 5, 1995). http://www.holyseemission.org/contents/statements/address-of-his-holiness-john-paul-ii-1995.php.

Part 4

Judaism, Christianity, and the West: Building and Preserving the Institutions of Freedom

10

ZIONIST THOUGHT ON ECONOMIC LIBERTY

Zev Golan

A consideration of Zionism within the framework of a conference on religion and economic liberty is apt, though at first glance it may seem out of place for at least two reasons. First, Zionism is a political or revolutionary movement, not a religious one. Second, Zionism is perceived by almost everyone as socialist in its beginnings and statist in its development and current form.

As to the first point, Zionism is clearly the Jewish people's and Jewish culture's most important development and accomplishment of at least the past century or two, if not millennium. As such, if Judaism is alive today, Zionism is its face. The Jewish people were given by God and long ago gave the world the faith of Abraham; the kingdom of David; the psalms of David; the wisdom of Solomon; the indignation of Isaiah and Jeremiah; and the beauty and mysteries of the Talmud, the Midrash, and the Kabbala. The most recent such gift is a political movement that embodies the divine spirit and passion of the Jewish people; a return to history after centuries of ghettos, inquisitions, and pogroms; a return to the land; and a return, in many respects—some that have yet to be actualized—to God.

As for Zionism's socialist image, one might draw a parallel to Samuel Gregg's introduction to Rabbi Joseph Lifshitz's book *Judaism, Law and the Free Market*. Gregg writes that Lifshitz does not make an exaggerated claim that Judaism favors a market economy. Instead, Lifshitz notes that some Jewish religious figures did address issues of property; exchange; economic justice; charity, and, based on their writings, it would be difficult to reconcile Judaism with social democracy.¹

Similarly, it would be absurd to claim that Zionism as a movement has supported markets. On the contrary, it is part of the Jewish tragedy that in the decades preceding the creation of the State of Israel so much energy went into efforts to liberate the working class instead of the homeland and its resident Jews and the desperate Jews of Europe.² Zionism, however, had liberal (i.e., liberty-loving) trends that moved Jewish history forward before socialists piggybacked on those trends and, in some cases, proceeded to undo their predecessors' accomplishments. Thus, the same seemingly eternal conflict between liberty and equality, independence and dependence, and the individual and collectivism that exists wherever there are people, exists also in Zion.

To paraphrase Gregg's introduction to Lifshitz, some Zionist figures did address issues of property, economic justice, and charity, and they concluded that Zionism would do well to have a basis in economic liberty. As noted, some of these people made important contributions to Zionism and changed the face of the Land of Israel.

THE FIRST POLITICAL ZIONIST

The man who may have been the first modern political Zionist, Rabbi Hyam Sneersohn, preceded Theodor Herzl by over a quarter of a century. Both called for solving the problems of Eastern Europe's persecuted Jews by establishing a Jewish state in Palestine. Both fought against philanthropy, arguing instead for investment. Both even founded banks for this purpose. Sneersohn left Jerusalem to travel around the world to raise money to buy *Batei Machsa*, a complex of homes to house the poor Jews of Jerusalem. He thought his best selling point was that his listeners should see their funding

---

¹ Joseph Isaac Lifshitz, *Judaism, Law, and the Free Market* (Grand Rapids: Acton Institute and JIMS, 2012).

² Dr. Israel Eldad, a Jewish underground leader in the 1940s and later a philosopher, often noted that the *Times of London* of November 9, 1917, had two headlines opposite each other on one page: "Palestine for the Jews," announcing the Balfour Declaration, and "Coup D'état in Petrograd," announcing that Lenin had deposed Kerensky. The Jewish youth of the time, and especially the large number of Jewish youth in Russia and its satellites, were offered two choices. All too many committed their lives to and died for Socialism rather than for Zion.

not as charity but as a real-estate investment that they would be able to realize at any time. When he traveled around the world, had had audiences with US President Ulysses S. Grant and other leaders. Later, back in Palestine, he organized a petition that was signed by fifty-seven poor Jews in Tiberias and sent to Jewish newspapers. It opened with a reference to Genesis 3:19: "We the undersigned are desirous to cultivate the land of our fathers, that we may earn our livelihood by the sweat of our brow."[3] But the old guard in Tiberias preferred charity to work and productivity.

When the former governor of Florida Jeb Bush suggested in July 2015 that Americans "have to be a lot more productive, workforce participation has to rise ... people need to work longer hours," Joseph Sunde titled his Acton blog "Jeb Bush Says Work Harder; Americans Respond By Complaining."[4] However, Bush got off easy. Those holding the keys to the charity boxes in Tiberias claimed that Rabbi Sneersohn had messianic delusions. They stripped him naked, tied him to a donkey, and ran him out of town.[5]

Sneersohn's timing was not right; five-dozen men in Tiberias were not yet the masses Herzl would inspire. The plight of Eastern Europe's Jews was bad, but the world had not yet seen the pogroms of 1881 in Russia that started the mass aliyah of Jews setting off to join their brethren already in Palestine, nor the Dreyfus affair that showed that the West, too, was no safe haven for Jews.

THE FOUNDER OF THE ZIONIST MOVEMENT

Two people gave expression to the Jewish spirit, the Jewish historical genius, and changed the Jewish people by restoring to them the sense of pride and

---

[3] Hyam Zvee Sneersohn, *Palestine and Roumania* (1872; repr., New York: Arno Press, 1977), 119–20.

[4] Joseph Sunde, "Jeb Bush Says Work Harder; Americans Respond By Complaining." Acton Institute PowerBlog, July 16, 2015, http://blog.acton.org/archives/80182-jeb-bush-says-work-harder-americans-whine-about-jobs-and-wages.html.

[5] Jewish commentators offer many explanations for why Zachariah 9:9 has the Messiah riding on a donkey rather than on a speedy horse or in a royal carriage. Sneersohn's fate suggests that perhaps the donkey is not the Messiah's chosen means of transportation; perhaps the harbinger of redemption is being mocked and run out of town.

destiny they once had, which had been deadened by ghettos, massacres, and poverty: Theodor Herzl and Zev Jabotinsky. Both were classical liberals.

Herzl is often described today as a socialist visionary. Nothing would have appalled him more. He opens his introduction to *The Jewish State*, his 1896 book that marked the beginning of the Zionist political movement, with praise for "the spirit of enterprise, " noting that "all our material welfare has been brought about by men of enterprise," and adding, "I feel almost ashamed of writing down so trite a remark."[6] He writes of "private property, which is the economic basis of independence," and plans for it to be "developed freely and be respected by us."[7] He hopes that "it will soon become fashionable [in Palestine] to live in beautiful modern houses,"[8] so that the less well off would be inspired to strive to increase their earnings. Like Sneersohn, he, too, expected to raise capital from banks in the form of investments rather than relying on charity. Recognizing the danger governments pose to personal liberty, Herzl argued that "individual enterprise must never be checked by the Company [running the Zionist project] with its superior force."[9]

AFTER HERZL

Few Zionist leaders after Herzl accomplished as much as Zev Jabotinsky. Jabotinsky was a poet, playwright, and novelist. He founded the Jewish Legion within the British army during World War I to help take Palestine from the Turks. He founded the Haganah self-defense force in Jerusalem in 1920, to protect the city's Jews during Arab attacks. In April of that year, when Arabs did attack, he and nineteen of his soldiers were arrested by the British for possessing arms and were sentenced to prison—the first Zionist political prisoners in Palestine. During the 1930s, Jabotinsky became the Supreme Commander of the Irgun militia and gave impetus to the illegal

---

[6] Theodor Herzl, *The Jewish State*, available on Project Gutenberg, http://www.gutenberg.org/files/25282/25282-h/25282-h.htm#The_Jewish_State, leaf 73.

[7] Herzl, *The Jewish State*, leaf 116.

[8] Herzl, *The Jewish State*, leaf 109.

[9] Herzl, *The Jewish State*, leaf 116. I am devoting less space here to Herzl than to Jabotinsky because I elaborated on Herzl at an earlier conference. Zev Golan, "Religion and Economic Liberty" (paper presented at the Centennial of Milton Friedman's Birth, Jerusalem Institute for Market Studies ([JIMS], May 2012).

immigration of Jews from Europe to Palestine, despite the British blockade. He spent his last years warning of an impending Holocaust and died in 1940.

In a song composed in 1932, Jabotinsky wrote, "Out of the pit of decay and dust, with blood and sweat, will rise a generation, proud, generous, and fierce."[10] Jabotinsky actually raised the downtrodden and gave them hope. His biographer Samuel Katz told me this was Jabotinsky's greatest accomplishment: liberating the spirit of millions of East European Jews. Herzl had had the same effect on the Jewish world. Jews everywhere were made proud to be Jewish; Herzl united them, made them a nation again, and gave them a flag. Jabotinsky turned them into the freedom fighters of the 1930s and 1940s.[11]

Jabotinsky addressed the question of economic liberty some twenty-five years after Herzl had, but Jabotinsky based his own economic theory on the Bible. He cited Leviticus 23:22 and Exodus 20:9 (KJV).

> And when ye reap the harvest of your land, thou shalt not make clean riddance of the corners of thy field when thou reapest, neither shalt thou gather any gleaning of thy harvest: thou shalt leave them unto the poor, and to the stranger: I am the Lord your God.

> But the seventh day is the Sabbath of the Lord thy God: in it thou shalt not do any work, neither thou, nor thy son, nor thy daughter, thy man-servant, nor thy maid-servant, nor thy cattle, nor thy stranger that is within thy gates.

Following two verses from the final chapter of Leviticus (27:30, 32) stating that tithes are "holy unto God," he then cited Leviticus 25:10 (KJV):

> And ye shall hallow the fiftieth year, and proclaim liberty throughout all the land unto all the inhabitants thereof: it shall be a jubilee unto you; and ye shall return every man unto his possession, and ye shall return every man unto his family.[12]

---

[10] Zev Jabotinsky, "Shir Betar," see http://www.hebrewsongs.com/song-shirbetar.htm.

[11] For more on Jabotinsky, see Shmuel Katz, *Lone Wolf* (New York: Barricade Books, 1996). For the specifics of Jabotinsky's defense of Jerusalem and his connection to the Irgun, see Zev Golan, *Free Jerusalem* (Israel: Devora, 2003).

[12] Zev Jabotinsky, "The Jubilee Idea (1930)," in *Nation and Society: Selected Essays* (Tel Aviv: Shilton Betar, 1958), 37–38 [original in Hebrew].

According to Jabotinsky, the Bible's approach can be divided into three main categories or concepts: the Sabbath; *Pe'ah*, the corners of the field and agricultural gleanings; and the Jubilee.

The first two categories, the Sabbath and *Pe'ah*, provide protection for employees and a safety net for the poor, respectively. Along with the concept of tithing, which arranges for taxation, they put limits on work hours and conditions and assure general welfare. The Jubilee is an occasional leveling of the playing field.

Jabotinsky drew two conclusions from the biblical citations above. The first is that they lead to something not far from what we would call a welfare state. Thus, Jabotinsky's economic program adopted the view that society should provide a minimum amount of food, health care, and so forth to everyone. His second, analytical, conclusion is a greater insight into the Bible's approach. Jabotinsky says that, taken together, the biblical injunctions create a system in which freedom reigns—the freedom to succeed or to fail—between the Jubilee years. There are but two limits to the freedom, or two palliatives, and these are meant to prevent the poor from becoming destitute.

Jabotinsky concludes that the whole system is one of limited government. He takes pains to note that it is the opposite of socialism. It is based on preserving competition. According to Jabotinsky, the Sabbath, tithing, laws allocating gleanings and the corners of the field to the poor, and the Jubilee, adjust rather than prevent economic freedom.

> The biblical program has nothing in common with a prophylactic system that prevents any possibility of inequality, exploitation, competition, and economic struggle, before they happen. The Bible seeks to preserve economic freedom but also tries to adjust it with mini-reservations and medicines.[13]

The Bible, he stresses, was not legislating equality. He writes:

> The success of our project, as everyone knows, depends on including private property. And the nature of private property is also known to all: it goes where it can profit. Whether this is good is irrelevant, terms such as good and evil are irrelevant; this is simply the nature of things.[14]

---

[13] Jabotinsky, "The Jubilee Idea," in *Nation and Society*.

[14] Zev Jabotinsky, "Class," *Betar*, 1:123–30, chap. 4 [original in Hebrew].

True, he said, the Bible is full of social protest—but not socialism. He termed the give and take of economics a game. It is critical, he said, not to interfere in the game. People need to be able to try to amass more wealth, to develop, and to create. What matters in the game are the incentives, and these must be preserved. Only a market economy allows for play and competition, and therefore state involvement should be minimized.[15]

Comparing socialism to this system, Jabotinsky calls it censorship versus freedom of speech with laws to ensure that speech does not overstep certain bounds; or a prohibition of rallies versus freedom of assembly with police stationed nearby in case something goes awry.[16]

Jabotinsky writes of the Bible's "wishing to combat poverty and seeking to eliminate it," but argued, "there is no connection and no bridge between this desire and a 'proletarian' class outlook."[17] He states that bourgeois capitalism is a system that can be stable, adjust itself, and make corrections; it has within itself the seeds of social ideals worthy of dreaming and fighting for.[18]

In terms of his own proposal to reinstitute the Jubilee, Jabotinsky taught that the Bible set forth its ideas in general terms, and he hints that he is not sure that the Jubilee was ever observed as written. Thus, when he came to propose a similar plan for today, he took care to say he wanted to apply the Bible's message with flexibility, not necessarily requiring Jubilee every fifty years or at any predetermined period. His idea was to institute a plan for times of crisis. Nor did he lay out the means of declaring Jubilee. He suggested referendums, a congress, or any other means as long as it was set by law in advance. Additionally, he warned always to be careful that, regardless of the form the Jubilee takes, the institution of credit be protected.[19]

---

[15] Zev Jabotinsky, "Introduction to Economic Thought" (1933), in *Nation and Society*, 49–56. See also Uri Heitner, "The Political and Social Thought of Jabotinsky," November 2010 [original in Hebrew], available at http://israblog.nana10.co.il/blogread.asp?blog=272685&blogcode=12149650.

[16] Jabotinsky, *Nation and Society*, 39.

[17] Jabotinsky, "Class," chap. 3.

[18] Jabotinsky, *Nation and Society*, 40.

[19] Jabotinsky, *Nation and Society*, 39.

The Fate of Liberal Zionism

Rabbi Sneersohn was driven from Tiberias. Others were driven from the Zionist movement. After Chaim, Weizmann took over the movement and turned Herzl's political Zionism into what he called synthetic, more practical, Zionism. One of the first to go was Herzl's deputy, Max Nordau, whose crime was calling for a mass exodus of hundreds of thousands of Jews from Europe before disaster befell them. The next to go was Louis Brandeis, the US Supreme Court justice, who believed in basing the building of Palestine on investment not charity. Later Jabotinsky went into political exile because he called (in 1931) for a Jewish state and Jewish army, which the Labor movement was not yet willing to promote. Weizmann and many others remade the Zionist movement into a philanthropic organization living off the kindness of nations and strangers.

Were such relative liberals as Jabotinsky, and to some extent Brandeis and his associates, short-lived comets? Did they have no influence?

True, Weizmann and David Ben-Gurion took over, but by the late 1920s, they turned Herzl's tools over to non-Zionists. Entrepreneurship-minded leaders such as Brandeis were sidelined. Entrepreneurs such as Pinchas Rotenberg, the founder, builder, and owner of the Electric Corporation, and Moshe Novomeyski of the Dead Sea Works, built the country and had their plants nationalized in the 1950s.

Jabotinsky's views on economics, and his commitment to individualism, were of great importance for the Zionist movement. They were an alternative to socialist Zionism. As such, they allowed many nonsocialists to find a home in Zionism and then in Zion. They assured that most of the tens of thousands of members of Jabotinsky's youth movement, Betar, would absorb and later espouse views favoring markets. Many of these people were the builders of Israeli cities, industries, and homes.

Jabotinsky's top student was Menachem Begin. He was the Commander in Chief of the Irgun during its war for independence from England in 1944–1948. He was elected prime minister in 1977. As prime minister, Begin fought entrenched interests and socialist parties to liberalize the economy.

Begin referred to the rights to life, liberty, work, and the pursuit of happiness. His explanation for his approach was that he based it on the Bible's statement that man—all persons of all religions, nationalities, and races—is created in God's image.[20]

---

[20] Moshe Fuksman-Shaal, "The Economic Revolution in Israel—From Socialism to a Free Market," *Hauma* 174 (2008): 26 [original in Hebrew].

Begin said:

> Once, at a time when liberal thought blossomed, there was a saying that the authorities of the state should be limited to those of a night watchman. That time has passed, but every free man prays in his heart that we won't have to say it has passed forever.[21]

The socialist party and bureaucracy that ruled Israel with a heavy hand was not the same after Begin's premiership.

A Normative Lesson

There is a telling trait that Herzl, Jabotinsky, and Begin shared, and it has normative implications for a discussion of the place of religion, or of liberty, in Zionism and the state of Israel. They personified challenges. Win or lose, their selves expressed their truths. Herzl challenged the whole Jewish world and changed it. Jabotinsky did the same and lost his political power, but he still changed the Jewish world. Louis Brandeis challenged the system and he, too, lost, but Brandeis' business-based loans helped build cities such as Herzliya and Natanya (the latter named for US businessman Nathan Straus). If those struggling for liberty or if a religion appears in society as an interest group seeking relief, lower taxes, or benefits such as budgetary allocations and exemptions from antireligious policies, then the state essentially controls it and determines its fate and how far it can go. People with ultimate values would do better to keep them ultimate. Professor Yeshayahu Leibowitz wrote that religion is not a tool to realize socialism or capitalism; for believers, religion is the ultimate goal.[22]

Freedom, too, is not something to barter over or to beg for more of within the context of statist socialism. Freedom, like religion, is an ultimate. (Obviously each person decides for himself, which is his ultimate.) By their character and essence, they are both ultimate values and need to be challenges to wayward society.

---

[21] Fuksman-Shaal, "The Economic Revolution in Israel," 25, citing Begin in a Knesset speech, 7 February 1950.

[22] Yeshayahu Leibowitz, "The Socio-Political Reality as a Religious Problem (1947)," in *Yahadut, Am YehudiUmedinat Israel* (Jerusalem: Schocken, 1979), 98–100 [original in Hebrew].

11

NATURAL LAW IN JUDAISM REVISITED

*Santiago Legarre**

In his book *Natural Law in Judaism*, David Novak successfully uncovered the presence of natural law in the Old Testament.[1] I am not an expert on Jewish contributions to natural law theory; consequently, I will rely heavily on Rabbi Novak's learned account with regard to the Jewish sources discussed in this chapter. For my part, I will explore instead the classical natural law tradition from Aristotle (before Christ) to Aquinas (in the Middle Ages) to John Finnis (in the twentieth century).

Abiding by the motto *non multa sed multum*, instead of trying to cover a myriad of topics that are relevant to the ways in which natural law theory can contribute to the understanding of freedom, I will focus on one. That one is the relevance of the connection between natural law and the positive laws—what is known in the classical tradition as the "derivation of positive from natural law." I will use Novak's argument as my starting point. I will try to develop it further by applying a crucial distinction in the thought of Thomas Aquinas—between the two modes of derivation of human, positive law from natural law—to the two ways in which natural law is present in the positive law of God.

---

* The author wishes to thank Gregory Mitchel and Christophe Rico for insightful comments.

[1] David Novak, *Natural Law in Judaism* (1998; repr., Cambridge, UK: Cambridge University Press, 2008).

Natural Law before the Covenant

I often wonder where some now-famous expressions come from. Was nothing "taken seriously" until Ronald Dworkin published his first book, *Taking Rights Seriously*? Did Evelyn Waugh patent revisits when he wrote his novel *Brideshead Revisited*? Whatever the answer, I find myself, now and then—like many others—using expressions such as these. I have borrowed from Waugh before[2] and I shall do so again here as I choose to title this contribution "Natural Law in Judaism Revisited."

Novak's pioneer visit to natural law in Judaism, in my view, makes three crucial moves. First, Novak defines natural law. Second, he insists that a natural law perspective may be present even if it is not referred to by name. Third, with the former in mind he identifies instances of natural law in the early part of what we Christians call the Old Testament.

What is meant by natural law or law of nature? In order to define natural law, it is important to understand that this notion predates Christianity. It is well known that the idea of natural law was present in the pre-Christian Greek philosophers, most notably Plato and Aristotle. Novak defines natural law as "those norms of human conduct that are universally valid and discernible by all rational persons."[3] This definition is not far removed from one given by Sophocles in *Antigone*. We surely recall her famous words about the unwritten laws of Hades, which apply *mutatis mutandis* to natural law: "their life is not of today or yesterday, but from all time, and no man knows when they were first put forth."[4]

At the dawn of the Christian era, at a time when it was only just becoming possible to speak of Christianity, one significant Christian—a man who had been a Jew for the majority of his life[5]—preached and affirmed natural law. I refer, of course, to Saul of Tarsus—Rabbi Saul to the Jewish people

---

[2] I borrowed Waugh's expression in my article "Derivation of Positive from Natural Law Revisited," *American Journal of Jurisprudence* 57 (2012), 103–10, on which I rely partly in section 2 below.

[3] Novak, *Natural Law in Judaism*, 1.

[4] Sophocles, *Antigone*, trans., E. H. Plumptre, Harvard Classics (New York: P. F. Collier & Son 1909–1914), vol. 8, pt. 6, line 500. On natural law's universality, see John Finnis, *Natural Law and Natural Rights*, 2nd ed. (1980; repr., Oxford: Oxford University Press, 2011), §§3–5.

[5] As Paul says in the New Testament, "I am a Jew, from Tarsus in Cilicia," Acts 21:39 NIV.

and later known as Saint Paul. In chapter 2 of his *Letter to the Romans* he famously states:

> So, when gentiles, not having the [Jewish] Law, still through their own innate sense [i.e., natural law] behave as the Law commands, then, even though they have no [Jewish] Law, they are a [natural] law for themselves. They can demonstrate the effect of the [natural] Law engraved on their hearts, to which their own conscience bears witness; since they are aware of various considerations, some of which accuse them, while others provide them with a defense. Rom. 2:14–15 NJB

As I have attempted to indicate with my bracketed insertions, we find in Paul's description all the various elements of natural law.

Returning to Novak, his definition is also compatible and in line with Thomas Aquinas who famously stated that "natural law is nothing else than the rational creature's participation of the eternal law."[6]

It is worth noting that, as explained by the Chilean philosopher Cristóbal Orrego, "natural" in "natural law" "does not mean related to the physical world but rather related to the rational world of human morality. Hence, the distinction between merely conventional morality and critical morality also captures the basic idea that some things may be morally good, and just, regardless of social conventions to the contrary."[7] Although not without its own ambiguities, the phrase "objective critical morality" can therefore replace natural law in some contexts.

Note that my classical concept of natural law commits to moral cognitivism. Furthermore, it is compatible with (and indeed requires) the respect of the positivity of man-made written laws. When we revisit the derivation thesis, I will comment more on this.

Second, Novak stresses that the question of natural law—as well as the related question of whether natural law is present in the Old Testament—is not a question of names. One of the strengths of Novak's approach to natural law is indeed that he realizes that one can talk about natural law

---

[6] Thomas Aquinas, *Summa Theologiae* (*ST*), 1–2, q. 91, a. 2c.

[7] Cristóbal Orrego, "The Relevance of the Central Natural Law Tradition for Cross-Cultural Comparison: Philosophical and Systematic Considerations," in *Natural Law and Comparative Law*, ed. Russell Wilcox and Anthony Carty (London: Wildy, Simmonds & Hill, 2012), 42.

under "whatever name."⁸ The "natural law under whatever name" idea has been successfully applied in different contexts.⁹ It is also important when it comes to tracing the presence of natural law in Judaism. Let me share with you what happened to me during breakfast the day I arrived in Jerusalem for the conference. I had breakfast with a Christian scholar, a student of the Jewish Bible who had resided in Israel for the previous twenty years. When I told him I had come to Jerusalem to speak about natural law in Judaism he looked at me perplexed: "It seems rather obvious that there is no such thing as natural law in the Old Testament," he exclaimed. Indeed there is no such thing *called* natural law in the Old Testament, but the relevant question is: Is there *such a thing* in the Old Testament, regardless of its label? My answer, like Novak's, is in the affirmative.

Professor John Finnis gave a piece of methodological advice to research students at the University of Oxford, which sheds light on this crucial distinction between the thing and its name(s): "The tools of our trade are propositions and meanings, statements and words. Get clear about these."¹⁰ Different words can have the same meaning (or concept or, ultimately, be the same thing);¹¹ two statements can convey the same proposition (ultimately, "the same thing"). I think all this is implicitly in place when Novak embarks on his formidable enterprise of tracing the presence of natural law in the Old Testament. Novak argues that the Jewish theologians who endorse the concept of natural law in Judaism "think that without this concept (*by whatever name it happens to be called* at different times in Jewish history), Judaism

---

⁸ Novak, *Natural Law in Judaism*, 1.

⁹ Orrego, for example, has applied it to the presence of natural law (under whatever name) in analytical positivism. See generally Cristóbal Orrego, "Natural Law Under Other Names: 'De Nominibus Non Est Disputandum'," *American Journal of Jurisprudence* 52 (2007): 77–92. I have applied it to the presence of natural law (under whatever name) in comparative constitutional analysis. Santiago Legarre, "Towards a New Justificatory Theory of Comparative Constitutional Law," *Strathmore Law Journal* 1 (2015): 107–12.

¹⁰ John Finnis, "Research Methodology in Jurisprudence," University of Oxford (2004). Photocopy.

¹¹ I have played with this methodological tool, distinguishing the term from the concept of police in my article, "The Historical Background of the Police Power," *University of Pennsylvania Journal of Constitutional Law* 9 (2007): 745.

would have no place for human reason."[12] "Concept" here—the equivalent of "meaning" in Finnis's rendition of the same—is rightly distinguished from "word" (or "name").

Another instance of the smart use of the distinction between concepts and words in Novak's work is when he asserts that the fifteenth-century Spanish Jewish theologian Joseph Albo introduced the term (i.e., the word or name) *natural law* into Jewish theology "but not the concept."[13]

Third, Novak traces the presence of the concept of natural law—regardless of the name—in the Old Testament. He puts forward a general argument and subsequently illustrates the argument with several textual examples. The gist of the general argument is that even before a law—*the* Law (the Torah)—was given by God to Moses (i.e., promulgated[14]) some actions were already wrong (and, by implication, others were right). Furthermore, this wrongfulness (and rightfulness) could be known by the human being, a manifestation of which was the guilt experienced by the performer of that action who was held by God to be a sinner—someone who had trespassed some kind of norm. This norm, however, could not be the positive law of God because, by definition, in the period of time examined by Novak (the pre-Torah time) such positive law did not exist. Therefore, he concludes, there must be some other law that was being infringed: that is, natural law.

Novak offers a number of examples, in chronological order, starting with perhaps the clearest one of Cain and Abel. "The act [of murder]," argues Novak, "is one for which God holds him [Cain] guilty irrespective of why he actually did it. For it is the nature of the object or victim of the act that is morally determinative, not whatever subjective rationalization the perpetrator of the act might have come up with." Cain is held guilty of breaching a commandment—Novak frames the commandment as "Do no harm to one another"—that had not been explicitly enacted by God. The commandment could have been discerned by Cain regardless of that enactment for it had been written on his heart (metaphorically speaking). He is held guilty of the trespass "for an act God expects [him] to already know to be a crime."[15]

---

[12] Novak, *Natural Law in Judaism*, 27, emphasis added. He further notes that "[t]he absence of this concept [of natural law] would make human reason superfluous," 27.

[13] Novak, *Natural Law in Judaism*, 124.

[14] See Thomas Aquinas, *Summa Theologiae* (*ST*), I–II, q. 90, a. 4c.

[15] Novak, *Natural Law in Judaism*, 33–37.

The same is true of the other insightful Old Testament examples of wrongful conduct that follow in *Natural Law in Judaism*. They deal, among other topics, with sex and violence (during the "generation of the flood" and later with the rape of Dinah, Jacob's daughter); sodomy (the famous story of Sodom and Gomorrah); and lying (Abraham and Abimelech). As Novak points out, these are all "incidences that took place before the giving of the Torah at Mount Sinai.... What they indicate ... is that the normative *content* of the Sinai covenant need not be regarded as originally instituted at the event of the Sinai revelation."[16] In other words, the moral substance of what was later revealed (as opposed to or, rather, distinguished from the cultic aspects of that revelation) was already accessible by human beings before the covenant. That content was natural law.

Ratification and Determination of Natural Law in the Covenant

Now let us move—as if in a chronology within the Old Testament—to the post-covenant period. I will suggest in this section that within the covenant it is important to distinguish between different degrees of presence of natural law. If it is true, as Novak says, that the normative content of the Sinai covenant need not be regarded as originally instituted at the Sinai revelation, it is indeed true only about some aspects of that normative content. While the commandments to which these aspects refer—or rather the content of those commandments—preexisted the covenant, some other commandments—let us call them "cultic" for the sake of simplification—were actually instituted at the event of the Sinai revelation. To understand this distinction, I suggest that Thomas Aquinas's theory of derivation of positive from natural law will be helpful. First, let us refresh ourselves on Aquinas's view.

Aquinas's account of the relationship of natural law to positive law has a general theory: every just human law is derived from the law of nature. Or in the words of the sixteenth-century English lawyer Christopher St. German, quoted by John Finnis: "[i]n every law positive well made is somewhat of the law of reason."[17] The general theory has two, subordinate theorems:

---

[16] Novak, *Natural Law in Judaism*, 60, emphasis added.

[17] See Finnis, *Natural Law and Natural Rights*, 281.

derivation is always either *per modum conclusionis* or *per modum determinationis*.[18] I will refer to these as sub-theorems.

According to the first sub-theorem "*something* may be derived from the natural law ... as a conclusion from premises."[19] Aquinas provides an example: "that *one must not kill* may be derived as a conclusion from the principle that *one must do harm to no one*."[20] This first sub-theorem is called "derivation by way of conclusion."

The other sub-theorem is "derivation by way of determination" and, according to Aquinas, "it is likened to that whereby, in the arts, general forms are particularized as to details. Thus, the craftsman needs to determine the general form of a house to some particular shape."[21] Samuel Gregg gives an example in the twenty-first century:

> Legislators will understand ... that ... responsibility to protect human life requires them to implement a traffic system that protects motorists' lives. But a uniquely correct traffic system *cannot* be derived from the natural law. A number of arrangements, each of which has incommensurable advantages and weaknesses, may be consistent with the natural law. Hence, governments and courts must move here, *not by deduction*.[22]

---

[18] The idea of a general theory and a subordinate theorem I borrow from Finnis, *Natural Law and Natural Rights*, 285. Both the theory and the two sub-theorems are compressed in Aquinas, *Summa Theologiae* (*ST*), I–II, q. 95, a. 2c, conventionally titled "Whether every human law is derived from the natural law?" See also I–II, q. 95, a. 4c.

[19] Aquinas, *ST*, I–II, 95 a. 2c.

[20] Aquinas, *ST*, I–II, 95 a. 2c.

[21] Aquinas, *ST*, I–II, 95 a. 2c. This sub-theorem has been the object of more intense study. See for example Finnis, *Natural Law and Natural Rights*, 281–90; John Finnis, "The Truth in Legal Positivism," in *The Autonomy of Law*, ed. Robert P. George (Oxford: Clarendon Press, 1996), 201–3, 212–14 (now in *Collected Essays of John Finnis*, vol. 4, *Philosophy of Law* (Oxford: Oxford University Press, 2011), essay 7, 174–88); John Finnis, *Aquinas: Moral, Political, and Legal Theory* (Oxford: Oxford University Press, 1998), 266–70.

[22] Samuel Gregg, *Morality, Law, and Public Policy* (Sydney: St. Thomas More Society, 2001), 34, second emphasis added. Aquinas's own example is: "the law of nature has it that the evil-doer should be punished; but that he be punished in this or that way, is a determination of the law of nature." Aquinas, *ST*, I–II, 95 a. 2c.

Aquinas's division of the whole (human law) into two different parts (conclusions and determinations) has logical appeal. The theory claims that *all* human law is derived either *per modum conclusionis* or *per modum determinationis*.²³ The starting point of practical reasoning (derivation) is always an existing positive legal enactment—in both types of derivation. Therefore, in the homicide example (an example of derivation by way of conclusion), the starting point of the reasoning is a preexisting criminal-law enactment: the law of murder, a positive law.²⁴ The derivation of this positive law of murder from natural law by way of conclusion flows easily if one follows Aquinas's train of thought. The law of murder is a conclusion (deduction) from the moral precept "one must not kill," which is itself a conclusion from the more general principle of morality "one must do harm to no one."²⁵ Despite the potential for ambiguity, I use the word *conclusion* (as Gregg similarly uses *deduction*) as shorthand for the more proper expression *derivation by way of conclusion*.²⁶

One of Aquinas's main tenets is that some rules of human law (*conclusiones*) derive their moral import and binding force from natural law (even

---

²³ In Finnis's words: "[a]ny proper example (central case) of legal systems will be *positive law* in its entirety and all its parts." John Finnis, "Natural Law Theory: Its Past and Its Present" *American Journal of Jurisprudence* 57 (2012): 81, 94.

²⁴ Finnis has recently held that that part of the state's positive law consisting of *conclusiones* can be called natural law or *jus gentium* (law common to all peoples). Finnis, "Natural Law Theory," 81, 94. This is somewhat confusing. See Legarre, "Derivation of Positive from Natural Law Revisited," §2.

²⁵ In the above example (and in countless similar ones), there are two types of "derivation by way of conclusion" at work. First, a natural-moral precept is derived from a more general natural-moral principle (the moral prohibition of killing from the principle "one must do harm to no one"); second, a positive law is derived from the said natural-moral precept (the law of murder from the moral prohibition of killing). In this example, the first type of derivation by way of conclusion is thus "intra-moral;" the second one, instead, moves from the realm of morality into that of positive (or, as Aquinas more commonly says, human) law. Both types of derivation by way of conclusion are useful and readily used in moral, political, and legal theory.

²⁶ I hasten to clarify that the noun *conclusion* (or *deduction*) might suggest something false, aptly pointed out by Finnis: that the (broadly speaking legislative) act of positing is equivalent to deducing or announcing the conclusion of a deduction. See John Finnis, "Coexisting Normative Orders? Yes, but No," *American Journal of Jurisprudence* 57 (2012): 111, 112.

if they need, as they do, positivization), while others (*determinationes*) derive moral import and force only remotely from natural law, so much so that in the absence of a human rule there would be no obligation whatsoever: neither legal nor moral.[27]

To reiterate: *conclusiones* "owe their moral import partly to the fact that they pertain to the natural law."[28] Or, in Aquinas's old-fashioned, translated words: "*those things* which are derived in the first way [*conclusiones*], are contained in human law not as emanating therefrom exclusively, but have some force from the natural law also."[29] In modern words, the moral import of *conclusiones* is not (only) a consequence of their positivity but also of their independent (one could even say prior) moral content. In Finnis's words: "[s]ome positive laws [i.e., *conclusiones*] are also norms of the natural moral law."[30] With *determinations*, it is not so. Their moral import would not exist in the absence of their positivization. They have no independent, prior moral import. This is true, by the way, of the greater part of positive law, which consists of derivation by way of determination.

In the positive law of God, one can also find *conclusiones et determinationes*. It is true of the Torah, as it is also true of any just positive human enactment. It includes those commandments that have both an independent, prior moral import, that is, the divine law of murder (the Catholics' fifth commandment of the Old Testament) *and* cultic concretizations, of which examples abound, whose moral import would not exist in the absence of their positivization by God. We can already observe here the two ways in which natural law is present in the positive law of God and how they are not altogether different from those in which natural law is present in any just human law. With our human way of seeing things we can trace the first way to the wisdom of God and the second to the will of God. This takes us to another useful distinction recalled by Rabbi Novak.

---

[27] Thomas Aquinas put it thus: "those things which are derived in the second way have no other force than that of human law [*ex sola lege humana vigorem habent*]," *ST*, I–II, q. 95, a. 2c. Finnis tuned in to Aquinas's dramatic intensity: "This last statement really goes further than the analysis itself warrants." Finnis, *Aquinas*, 267 (where the justification for this observation is provided).

[28] Finnis, "The Truth in Legal Positivism," 202.

[29] Aquinas, *ST*, I–II, q. 95, a. 2c, emphasis added.

[30] Finnis, "The Truth in Legal Positivism," 202: "Some positive laws are also norms of the natural moral law—that is, are requirements of practical reasonableness."

Universal and Domestic Contents of the Law of God in Light of Derivation Theory

The distinction between *conclusiones* and *determinationes* is very much in line with a famous distinction recalled by Novak. This is between *mala in se* and *mala quia prohibita*. Novak links this latter distinction with the one between God's wisdom and God's will—and rightly so.[31] By coupling here both distinctions, I will continue to keep my initial promise of applying the thought of Thomas Aquinas on the two modes of derivation of positive law from natural law to the two ways in which natural law is present in the positive law of God.

In *determinatio* "whatever wisdom we perceive in [a Divine] commandment [or human enactment] is phenomenologically subsequent to our obedience of it."[32] In contrast, in *conclusio* with a commandment such as "you shall not murder, we can appreciate the wisdom of the commandment ... before we eventually understand that its prescription is part of God's wisdom."[33] Novak concludes about Judaism that this distinction explains why "Jews can speak persuasively in secular public space about the prohibition of murder in a way we cannot (and should not) speak of the prohibition of eating pork there." The case of murder is an example of the presence of derivation by way of conclusion in the law of God; the case of pork is an example of the presence of derivation by way of determination.[34] The same would be true for Catholics with the law of fasting: We cannot justify it in the secular public space in the same way we can speak of our religious laws against murder. Novak goes on:

> that is why the prohibition of murder is taken to be immediately universal, that is, rationally perceivable by all normal human persons capable of hearing it through nature. The prohibition of eating pork [or, for Catholics, the prohibition of eating meat during Lent], conversely, is

---

[31] Novak, *Natural Law in Judaism*, 16–18.

[32] Novak, *Natural Law in Judaism*, 17.

[33] Novak, *Natural Law in Judaism*, 17.

[34] At one of the conference dinners, one of the Jewish participants said to a group of us, as she was trying to explain the rules for kosher food: "It is capital that you don't try to find a rationale because there isn't one." To put it in Novak's terms, "God's will all over the place."

not immediately universal and requires, therefore, special revelation to a singular community in history.[35]

The distinction between *mala in se* and *mala quia prohibita*—and between *conclusiones* and *determinationes*—is also linked with the contrast between the universal, on the one hand, and the local and the domestic, on the other hand. Therefore, in the Old Testament, Laban retorts to Jacob that "to give the younger one before the older one in marriage is something not done *in our place.*"[36] In other words, "what you want is contrary to our local ordinance." It is "*mala quia prohibita*," as opposed to the rape of Dinah (Jacob's daughter, by a prince), which is something "not to be done" (*mala in se*).[37] Novak stresses the distinction between what is not to be done *simpliciter* and what is not to be done *in our place*. For example, when it comes to the commandment regarding rape as embodied later in divine-enacted law, the contrast between rape and certain marriages—analyzed by Novak in the light of the distinction between *mala in se* and *mala quia prohibita*—can be focused as well through the lens of derivation theory. Thus, the divine law prohibiting rape is derived by way of conclusion from natural law. Rape was wrong even before divine law promulgated its wrongfulness through a positive enactment—in this sense it was universally wrong—in a way analogous to that in which rape was wrong in a given community whose human laws prohibited it even before they decided to do so.

We can observe here a certain coexistence of two normative orders, one moral and one legal—the latter being human or divine depending on whether we focus on human positive law or divine positive law. In the theory of derivation, coexistence is never understood as in rationalistic accounts of natural law where two *separate* legal orders coexist; one natural; one positive.[38] Rather, for derivation theory, the coexistence of normative orders means pretty much what Finnis explained in *Natural Law and Natural Rights*. The

---

[35] Novak, *Natural Law in Judaism*, 18.

[36] Novak, *Natural Law in Judaism*, 50, emphasis added.

[37] Novak, *Natural Law in Judaism*, 51.

[38] J. M. Kelly, *A Short History of Western Legal Theory* (Oxford: Oxford University Press, 1992), 260: "Particularly in Germany, natural law was taken—of course in the secular sense which Grotius had given it—to be a material from which whole systems of municipal law could be fashioned" (commenting on the work of Pufendorf, Wolff, Vattel et al.).

law of murder—to stick to our example—"corresponds rather closely to the requirement of practical reason, which would be such a requirement *whether or not repeated or supported by the law of the land* [or by the positive law of God]: that one is not to deliberately kill the innocent."[39]

In his later work, Finnis reiterated this idea:

> [s]ome positive laws are also norms of the natural moral law that is, are requirements of practical reasonableness. But to say that is not to detract in the least from the positivity of those laws—that is from the fact (where it is the fact) that they have been posited humanly.[40]

In sum: If by a coexistence of two normative orders one understands two separate, complete codes that exist entirely separate from each other, then such a notion is useless. But the relationship of natural law to the positive law of a particular state *and*, analogously, to the positive law of God, is indeed one of interrelated coexistence. Insofar as natural law exists by way of conclusion and by way of determination in the positive law of a state *and*, analogously, in the positive law of God, it also continues to exist as a normative order independent of those legal orders, both in the practical reasoning of the addressees of the positive law and in the intelligence of the creator of that natural law[41]—which, in the case of divine positive law, is of course the same creative intelligence.

---

[39] Finnis, *Natural Law and Natural Rights*, 281, emphasis added.

[40] Finnis, "The Truth in Legal Positivism," 202–3.

[41] Aquinas, *ST*, I–II, q. 90, a. 1, ad. 1.

12

JUDAISM, NATURAL LAW, AND RELIGIOUS FREEDOM

Daniel Mark

HIGH DRAMA IN THE DESERT: THE EXISTENCE OF A HIGHER POWER

Before all the high drama of the Exodus—before the ten plagues, the splitting of the sea, the drowning of Pharaoh's army—there is a curious and often overlooked part of the episode that deserves our attention. In chapter 5 of the book of Exodus, Moses appears before Pharaoh to request a three-day furlough for the Israelite slaves to go worship their God in the wilderness. To us, who have read the book, this is rather strange. We know Moses is not planning a three-day prayer retreat; he is planning a full-scale escape. Moreover, if Moses is trying to trick Pharaoh into letting the people of Israel sneak away, the ruse is not very successful. Pharaoh, apparently suspicious of the request, says that the men can go but insists the women and children stay behind, knowing, of course, that the men will have to return at the end of the three days. Moses, naturally, declines the counterproposal. Therefore, our first question is why Moses asks in the first place. Is he lying? Does he think Pharaoh is that gullible? However, our second question is why Pharaoh even bothers to refuse. When the Israelites do finally flee, albeit with Pharaoh's blessing initially, Pharaoh merely has to send his army to round them up and bring them back. *We* know what happens when they reach the sea, but Pharaoh has no reason to worry about that at the stage that Moses makes his request (or at any stage thereafter until the miracle actually occurs). Why not let the Israelites go? They cannot escape, anyway, barring an unforeseen miracle.

I believe that a single insight explains both why Moses asks and why Pharaoh refuses. To allow the Israelites to go worship their God, even in this limited way, would be to acknowledge the existence and relevance of an authority beyond Pharaoh's own. It would be to admit that the Israelites do not belong wholly to Pharaoh, that they are subject to a higher power, and to introduce by implication the suggestion that perhaps everyone else is too. That is, it would be to concede that the Israelites are not *ultimately* subjects of the Egyptian god-king but of the transcendent God-King.

Although I am not a historian, I imagine that this idea is a significant feature of the great revolution that the Bible brought to the world. In the pagan world, a world in which the gods were the gods *of the city*, the state claimed everything for itself. To oppose the political order or the ruler was not only treason but also sacrilege. Then there came a new era: a time to render unto Caesar what was Caesar's but also to render unto God what was God's.

In America, we sometimes refer to religious freedom as the "first freedom." In part, this is because religious freedom appears first in the Bill of Rights. Religious freedom, though, is the first freedom in a deeper sense as well. The idea of religious freedom—the right to go worship God in the wilderness for three days—is where we first learn, conceptually and perhaps historically as well, the in-principle limits on the power of the state. The state cannot rightly dictate how to discharge our religious obligations, nor can the state countermand them. To answer to a higher authority is to mark out a realm of existence that is beyond the authority of the state.

More broadly, then, religious freedom teaches that our lives never belong wholly to the state. In understanding and securing religious freedom, we open the door to the full panoply of human rights and to the limits of the state. Therefore, in building and preserving the institutions of freedom in our time, we would do well to promote the centrality of religious freedom not only for its own sake but also because it undergirds all of our rights.

In this respect, Judaism has a role in the conceptual and perhaps even historical genesis of religious freedom. I would like to turn, however, to what Judaism can do for the promotion of religious freedom today. To address this question, I will consider three ways in which Judaism can contribute to the promotion of religious freedom and, by extension, to freedom in general.

I will roughly categorize these three ways, respectively, as philosophical, political, and theological.

Judaism's Philosophical Promotion of Religious Freedom

First, perhaps counterintuitively—and perhaps even paradoxically to the modern mind—Judaism has a philosophical contribution to make to the advancement of religious freedom because, in its ethos and its self-understanding, Judaism is focused far more on obligations than on rights. In an influential 1987 article, the late Yale legal philosopher Robert Cover wrote:

> The basic word of Judaism is obligation or mitzvah. It, too, is intrinsically bound up in a myth—the myth of Sinai. Just as the myth of social contract is essentially a myth of autonomy, so the myth of Sinai is essentially a myth of heteronomy. Sinai is a collective—indeed, a corporate—experience. The experience at Sinai is not chosen. The event gives forth the words which are commandments. In all Rabbinic and post Rabbinic embellishment upon the Biblical account of Sinai this event is the Code for all Law. All law was given at Sinai and therefore all law is related back to the ultimate heteronomous event in which we were chosen—passive voice.[1]

The central moment in Jewish history is the Exodus—the Israelites' liberation from their bondage in Egypt. The Exodus is recalled over and over in the Bible as the basis for so many injunctions: "Do such-and-such (or, do not do such-and-such) because you were once a slave in Egypt." Yet, the freedom obtained through the Exodus is not the culmination or fulfillment of the Israelites' liberation. Rather, that occurs at Sinai, as shown by the commandment to count the days and weeks from Passover to Pentecost, explicitly linking the Exodus, commemorated on Passover, to the revelation, or the giving of the Torah, at Mount Sinai, commemorated on Pentecost. God did not free the Israelites from Egypt so that they could become their own masters. God freed them so that they could be free to serve him, exchanging servitude to Pharaoh for servitude to him. In truth, a life of freedom is found in a life of service to God. The Jewish idea is that true freedom is found not in radical autonomy or antinomianism, which

---

[1] Robert M. Cover, "Obligation: A Jewish Jurisprudence of the Social Order," *Journal of Law and Religion* 5 (January 1987): 66.

provides merely the illusion of freedom, but in serving what is true and good. Our real liberation comes when we accept, as Jews say, the yoke of the kingdom of heaven.

Relatedly, Cover points out that while the language of duty is used throughout Scripture the Bible does not even have a word for rights. This is in stark contrast to our contemporary Western societies that place the greatest emphasis possible on rights, sometimes to their detriment.[2] We might say rather wryly that, alas, our modern culture is both obsessed with rights—everything I want is a right—and has lost sight of their proper ground and meaning. To be sure, this does not mean that Judaism or any serious view of truth and goodness is incompatible with the rights doctrines of classical liberalism. On the contrary, University of Toronto philosopher and theologian David Novak argues that the inherent dignity and equal worth of every human, embedded in the concept of *tzelem elokim* or *imago dei*, is the original source and ultimate and necessary justification for human rights.[3]

This does mean, though, that Judaism could contribute positively to the institutions of freedom in the West by helping us recover the centrality of obligations rather than rights in political life. The assault on religious freedom in the West has been largely abetted by our society's loss of the sense expressed in Cardinal Newman's dictum that conscience has rights because it has duties. When religious obligations are reduced to preferences—when religious freedom is reduced to freedom of choice, as Michael Sandel worries,[4] it becomes difficult to see why religious claims should stand in the face of other priorities. The protection of religious freedom is simply less urgent when one has no sense of what it means to be bound by religious obligations. Those obligations, as Newman taught, are the very reason religious freedom matters. I contend that religious freedom is being downgraded in this way not only because secular elites are increasingly estranged from the real meaning of religion but also because they

---

[2] See Mary Ann Glendon, *Rights Talk: The Impoverishment of Political Discourse* (New York: Free Press, 1991).

[3] David Novak, *Natural Law in Judaism* (1998; repr., Cambridge, UK: Cambridge University Press, 2008).

[4] See, for example, Michael J. Sandel, "Freedom of Conscience or Freedom of Choice?" in *Articles of Faith, Articles of Peace: The Religious Liberty Clauses and the American Public Philosophy*, ed. James Davison Hunter and Os Guinness (Washington, DC: Brookings Institution, 1990), 74–92.

are increasingly estranged from the concept of obligation altogether. The philosophical hedonism of our age, where desires are self-validating (that is, things are good merely because we desire them), reduces everything to choice, which is also why consent has become the overriding, almost exclusive, operating principle. Therefore, a robust recovery of the notion of obligation will actually buttress the notion of rights because the force of rights claims will become salient once again.

Now let me go a drop further with this point that Judaism has a contribution to make to freedom because of its emphasis on obligation. If the reintroduction of the notion of obligation is important, Judaism is especially well suited to do this because it is so centered on command and commandedness. Although plenty of obligations do not come from commands, authoritative commands are probably the simplest and clearest way for people to grasp the concept of obligation. The obligatoriness of the moral law, which involves obligations that were neither imposed on me by myself nor by someone else with the authority to do so, is harder to comprehend. Witness the almost universal view nowadays that I can never sin against myself. This is the consent doctrine again. Judaism says that the law must not interfere with my religious obligations because I am commanded to fulfill them. Judaism can well project this idea of commandedness because daily life, not to mention the arc of one's entire life, is so highly structured around the fulfillment of the commandments. Judaism represents a life of commandedness and therefore a life of obligation-fulfillment.[5]

At the same time, a reliance on commandedness to recover the notion of obligation presents its own obstacles. Although, in theory, commandments may be the surest conceptual route to obligation, that theme may speak weakly to a modern age where the idea of commandedness, to say nothing of a Commander, is terribly out of vogue. Indeed, a fair critic might suggest that the idea of commandments is as foreign today as is the idea of freestanding obligations not arising from my elective commitments. People today have a hard time relating to the idea of obligation, but they may have an even harder time relating to the idea of commandments. That is

---

[5] In a superficial way, I think this is more the case with Judaism than with Christianity. To be clear, I am not setting up a simplistic dichotomy between Judaism and Christianity that associates Judaism with obligation and Christianity with freedom from obligation or any such thing. Indeed, I am not even setting up Judaism and Christianity in opposition to each other in any strong way. It is more a matter of appearance or emphasis. Nor am I criticizing Christianity in this.

to say, even moderns operating in good faith with respect to morality may have a hard time being brought to the idea of obligation through the idea of commandedness.

Second, there is a deeper and more complicated problem that also abets the first issue. To speak of commandedness as being at the heart of Judaism is to have in mind traditional Judaism. Most Jews today, especially in America and Israel, do not fit that mold. My concern is that, even among Jews who continue to endorse the notion of commandedness, there is an absence of a natural law understanding of commandedness and of obligation more generally. Unfortunately, even David Novak, the preeminent contemporary Jewish natural law thinker, stops short of adopting, at bottom, a natural law basis for obligation; instead, he asserts the primacy of raw divine command. Novak thinks that our moral obligations, which come to us as religious obligations, ultimately rest on divine command and cannot be fully accounted for without that. This is problematic because divine command alone cannot account for the first religious obligation, namely the moral obligation to obey the divine command. There is no original divine command to obey divine commands, and, if there were, it would be recursive. Adam and Eve are commanded not to eat from the tree, but they are just supposed to know that they are obligated to obey that command. That obligation, of necessity, depends on a natural law account of the moral obligation to be in harmony with God if he exists. Novak's avoidance of this final step squares well with his assertion of *tzelem elokim* or *imago dei* as the ultimate ground for human dignity and equality, which he does not think can be constructed on natural law grounds alone. In both cases, I think his view falls short.

This leads, I fear, to a more voluntaristic and fideistic understanding of commandedness that, for one thing, lacks an account of why anyone outside the covenant has obligations—that is to say, why the moral law applies to those who did not receive the Law as well. That is problematic because it leaves Judaism without a notion of obligation that can be made meaningful to the rest of the world. It is true that Judaism believes there are a few commandments that God gave to the whole world. But the aim here is not to see whether Jews can convince the rest of the world that it has obligations to God but whether the Jewish *idea* of commandments that bind *the Jews themselves* is an idea that can be pedagogically useful to society without needing to export the commandments themselves. With an overly fideistic view of commandedness, the answer is probably no.

Therefore, in order for Judaism to make this important contribution of turning politics from its emphasis on rights to an emphasis on obligation, it must reconstruct for itself a fully coherent notion of commandedness and obligation. Before it can fruitfully bring those concepts back into the public square, Judaism must restore a natural law understanding of obligation that *explains* commandedness and does not just *depend* on it. I say "restore" because, in my view, this natural law understanding is built into the tradition, but I confess that few others see it that way.

JUDAISM'S POLITICAL PROMOTION OF RELIGIOUS FREEDOM

There is a different way, however, in which David Novak's thought indicates a Jewish contribution to religious freedom, which brings me to my second point: the political, by which I mean political theory, angle. In a great work entitled *The Jewish Social Contract*, Novak argues that the fundamental form of social identity is that of the community, as opposed to the individual or the society. A core tenet of Novak's work is that the community has what he calls historical and ontological priority over the individual and over society. For Novak, this is true as a descriptive matter, but it carries great normative weight as well because the priority of community not only makes the social contract possible but also ensures its viability and desirability.

A social contract between individuals is first and foremost impossible because such naked Rawlsian specimens simply do not exist. This is why the community has historical priority over the free, choosing individual. Novak writes:

> any contract between persons, be it a private contract or a public contract between all parties to the society and for the sake of the society, any such contract is not the most original or even the most persistent social bond, certainly not for Jews. Truly, without the presupposition of more original social or communal bonds, the idea of the social contract becomes incoherent since there are no real persons to come to it. Only full persons and not abstractions can contract with one another in any substantial way. Persons are social beings by nature, not by mutual agreement. There cannot be contracting persons, as distinct from humanoid phantoms, who are not already socialized.... Thus no contract between persons can create a primal community because a primal community, one's original society, hovers around persons before there are any real agreements between persons within it, much

less agreements between persons crossing over original borders and coming together from their different communities into a civil society.[6]

Moreover, a social contract built on individuals rather than on communities is unviable and undesirable because only a social contract between communities can resist the totalizing tendencies of the state. Standard liberal social contract theory also purports to protect rights, including religious freedom, although, to be sure, that has not provided a very firm basis for religious freedom a couple of centuries on. Nevertheless, for Novak, the covenantal community is the only sort of community that possesses the historical and ontological priority necessary for its claims truly to be rights claims and not merely special pleading. That is, only religious communities can make the sort of claims that keeps the state in check. The covenant with God is the source of the community's ontological priority. As Novak argues in another important book, *Covenantal Rights*, all rights and duties originate with God. For this reason, the rights of the community are both inviolable (from without) and inalienable (from within).[7] The community brings with it into civil society all of the rights it possesses before the creation of civil society. Civil society cannot abrogate those rights because it neither creates nor bestows them.

Novak argues that, when "a civil society no longer respects communal priority, it inevitably attempts to replace the sacred realm by becoming a sacred realm itself. That is, such a society attempts to become the moral authority over which there is no greater authority in the lives of its citizens." In this way, civil society becomes "civil religion," which "usurps the role of historic faith traditions and becomes what it was never originally intended to become: unlimited authority." The limitation of the range of government's authority is the "hallmark of a democratic social order," but this limitation "cannot come from within; it can only come from what is both outside it and above it." Novak continues, "external and transcendent limitation can be found in the freedom of citizens of a democracy to find their primal identity by being and remaining parts of their traditional communities. This is what has come to be known in democracies as 'religious liberty.'" For Jews, he concludes, "this means that their historical and ontological identity

---

[6] David Novak, *Jewish Social Contract: An Essay in Political Theology* (Princeton: Princeton University Press, 2005), 11–12.

[7] David Novak, *Covenantal Rights: A Study in Jewish Political Theory* (Princeton: Princeton University Press, 2009).

in God's covenant with the people of Israel is what both limits secularity and entitles its limited range to be beneficial for them. Judaism is both older and deeper than any civil society."[8]

Christians, too, hold a special place in Novak's thought. First, as he says, Christians are the only people with whom Jews can speak biblically. Jews and Christians share some of the same principles, such as man's being created in the image of God. Second, I infer that much of what Novak says about Jews with respect to civil society also applies to Christians because Christians consider themselves a covenantal community as well. In fact, the Hebrew phrase meaning New Testament, *brit chadasha*, equivalently means new covenant, using the same word (*brit*) that Jews use to describe their covenant with God.

One minor question can be raised concerning the extension of this entire conceptual apparatus from Judaism to Christianity. Novak understands civil society properly formed to be multicultural: a society composed entirely of minority groups. This does not mean that any one group must be a minority demographically, just politically in terms of the ideology and policies of the state. In this latter respect, Christianity probably qualifies, not because America today happens to be very secular and even anti-Christian but because the West has not been officially Christian since the fall of Christendom in the early modern period. Europe, which has remained officially Christian, has been nothing more than that.[9] One small doubt does creep in, though, because of Christianity's universalistic outlook, which Judaism does not share. Aspirationally, Christianity is not a minority religion or a minority culture. Therefore, a fair question ought to be asked about whether Christians can, as Jews can in principle (which is to say in good faith), sign on to Novak's multiculturalist project of a civil society comprised of minority communities.

A more difficult question we must confront is what Novak's ideas mean for individuals who do not identify with a primal community. The difficulty is not with what Novak would say about them—he is fairly clear on this subject—but whether their effective exclusion limits the utility of Novak's theory for our society. The escape hatch is that Novak thinks that people

---

[8] Novak, *Jewish Social Contract*, 9.

[9] For the record, I say this as someone who refers to America as a Christian country and means it as a compliment—though I should add that American Christianity is unique.

who reject their ancestral faith—those who are reared Jewish or Christian and walk away from it—do not really exit community altogether but instead leave one to join another. Yet Novak does consider the question of what is to be done about secularists and atheists, and the spirit of the question is reminiscent of Fr. Richard John Neuhaus's splendid article, "Can Atheists Be Good Citizens?"[10] How can atheists enter the social contract if the civil society is formed not by individuals but by covenantal communities? Where do they enter, and what inviolable, inalienable claims do they bring with them? According to Novak:

> it is easy to see why such avowed secularists cannot make any cultural claims on civil society that are not merely those of a human opinion group employing special pleading. Accordingly, they can only ask for entitlements from civil society, entitlements that civil society can take away from them as easily as it can give these entitlements to them. Denying historical and ontological priority, secularists must rely on social largesse inasmuch as they have no transcendent point of reference from which to truly demand human rights as prior claims.[11]

Novak does gesture toward a solution whereby he wishes to include all people who accept the authority of an absolute moral law, even if they are a bit queasy about theism. However, this does not really fulfill the requirement of community membership because there is no covenantal community of natural lawyers. In the end, we must accept that secularists and atheists only join civil society incidentally, though they do of course reap all the benefits of the limited state that is guaranteed by the participation of religious communities in the same civil society.

Quite explicitly for Novak, it is the participation of the Jewish community and similarly situated communities in the social contract that stands as the primary and indispensible bulwark against the tyranny of the state. I would say, for Novak it is *especially* the Jewish community, which is the paradigmatic biblical, covenantal, and minority community that so stands. The participation of these communities secures, above all, religious freedom because that is their chief concern and their chief reason for joining the social contract. Because Novak insists that religious communities can only fulfill this responsibility when they are authentic, when they are faith-

---

[10] Richard John Neuhaus, "Can Atheists be Good Citizens?" *First Things* 15 (August/September 1991): 17–21.

[11] Novak, *Jewish Social Contract*, 26.

ful to the covenant with the God who is the source of all rights and duties, religious freedom as a necessary condition for this faithfulness must be protected most of all. Thus, there is a symbiotic relationship between the protection of religious freedom and the flourishing of authentic religious communities within civil society, the former enabling the latter and the latter guaranteeing the former.

Judaism's Theological Promotion of Religious Freedom

The third mode in which Judaism can contribute to the advancement of religious freedom is theological. Judaism is not evangelical in the way that Christianity or Islam is (which is not to say that Christianity and Islam are evangelical in the same way). Judaism neither desires nor demands of non-Jews to become Jewish. On the contrary, prospective converts are gently discouraged and only accepted if they persist and then complete years of rigorous preparation. Even in the Jewish view of the messianic era, all the nations of the earth will recognize and worship the one true God, but they will do so *as the nations of the earth*, not as Jews.

What the Jewish tradition does expect from Gentiles is for them to be what is sometimes called "ethical monotheists." This means believing in the one true God and observing the so-called seven Noahide commandments, which the rabbis understand God to have given to Noah and his sons and, through them, to their descendants—the entire repopulated world. Some suggest that the seven Noahide commandments, which include prohibitions on murder, theft, illicit sex, animal cruelty, idolatry, and blasphemy and one affirmative requirement to set up courts to institute the rule of law, adumbrate the moral law—hence, the "ethical" part of ethical monotheists.[12]

Fulfilling their obligations to God through the Noahide law, Gentiles have no need to become Jewish. They do not need to convert in order to be saved (to use an exclusively Christian and definitely not Jewish term). Thus, in a deeply rooted theological way, Judaism permits and even encourages religious freedom because not only does Judaism not actively seek worldwide conformity to its faith, but it also does not contain even an underlying impulse for uniformity of belief. To be sure, I recognize that Christianity and particularly the Catholic Church has done much to promote religious

---

[12] For the connections between the Noahide law and natural law, see Novak, *Natural Law in Judaism*.

freedom as well. In fact, I would argue that *Dignitatis Humanae*, whose fiftieth anniversary we are celebrating, provides a firmer and more robust philosophical basis for religious freedom than anything of which I am aware in my admittedly inadequate knowledge of the Jewish tradition. Nevertheless, Judaism is fundamentally pluralistic in a way that I think Christianity and Islam are not because of the absence of an evangelical mandate, and this can help support an ethos of religious freedom. In our age, the defense of religious freedom requires not just toleration of diversity of belief but also validation of it.

One problem that you may have noted as I quickly listed the Noahide commandments is that idolatry is not permitted for Jews or Gentiles. This is not a practical problem for Jews in the West because the rabbis are generally of the opinion that we no longer have with us the full-on idolaters of antiquity. New York and Los Angeles may be pagan philosophically and culturally but not theologically. In any case, though, religious freedom in classical Judaism does not extend to idolaters. Jewish scholar Yoram Hazony has tried to explain how the eradication of idolatry can be publicly reasonable.[13] But, short of that argument, the Jewish concept of religious freedom, which excludes idolaters, remains narrower than the Western concept. My sense is that a good-faith pagan would fall under the umbrella of *Dignitatis Humanae* as well. Yet, this exception notwithstanding, I think the pluralism at Judaism's core adds more to the defense of religious freedom than Judaism's intolerance of idolatry subtracts.

Jewish Absence from the Promotion of Religious Liberty

To conclude, let me very briefly take up the question of why, despite these reasons, traditional Judaism today, unlike orthodox Christianity, has little voice in the debates over religious freedom.

First, the Jewish people have spent two thousand years learning to keep their heads down. The first rule of Jewish survival is not to attract any attention. In America—though probably only in America—this strategy may no longer be necessary, and it may even be shortsighted and counterproductive. The Jewish community, nevertheless, picks its battles very carefully, engaging actively and openly only on issues of the most vital concern—US policy

---

[13] Yoram Hazony, *The Dawn: Political Teachings of the Book of Esther* (Jerusalem: Shalem Press, 1995).

toward the State of Israel most prominently and issues such as government funding of parochial schools. One might ask, quite reasonably, why religious freedom does not rank near the top of this list as well. One reason is that ninety percent of the American Jewish community is not Orthodox, and, being wholly in sync with the prevailing culture, there is little prospect for conflict between their religion and the demands of the state with respect to abortion, gay marriage, and the like. On the other hand, the Orthodox, for whom conflict is inevitable, simply do not see it coming. There is one Jewish organization, not Orthodox but politically conservative, that is beginning to address this problem, but it is effectively the only Jewish organization doing serious work in this area.

Second, I have a thesis that the wide political and intellectual gap between Judaism and Catholicism today traces back to the fact that over the same two-thousand-year period, Judaism has developed a rich and complex legal tradition while Catholicism has developed a rich and complex philosophical tradition. Though there is far more to explore here than I can get into at this moment, each path of development has its advantages and disadvantages. The advantage to Judaism is that commitment to fulfillment of the law in all its detail remains rigorous. The disadvantage is that the neglect of the philosophical underpinnings of the tradition has left Judaism with much of who, what, when, where, and how but very little of why. The Jews' lack of a deep understanding of their own religious principles makes it very hard to carry those principles, to carry Jewish values, out into the public square. On what basis other than special pleading can Jews claim religious freedom and the right to be free of so many impositions of the state? This is why Judaism needs but does not have a *Dignitatis Humanae*, not to mention a *Humanae Vitae*.

In the end, the failure to promote ethical monotheism—the natural law—in the public square, whether for political or philosophical reasons, is first and foremost a failure of the Jewish mission, something Jews must learn from their "younger brothers in faith" who bravely and consistently witness to the mission of taking responsibility for the wellbeing not only of one's own community but also of one's society. It is, second of all, a strategic failure. Outside the Land of Israel, we Jews are destined to be strangers in a strange land. However, the way things are going in the West, Orthodox Jews will find out soon just how strange the Roman Empire can be without the civilizing influence of the Judeo-Christian ethic. For their own sake, and for the sake of the world, Jews must take up this fight.

13

Private Property, Religious Freedom, and Economic Development[*]

Michael Matheson Miller

Most discussions of economics and development tend to focus on economic indicators such as GDP or on themes such as infrastructure, education, and health care while neglecting more foundational issues. Infrastructure and health care are important, but these things are the *result* of wealth before they become the cause of it.

More foundational issues are private property, justice in the courts, the ability to register a business, and the ability to engage in economic activity without undue burden. Even deeper than this are the cultural and religious sources of these institutions—ways of seeing the world that shape our deepest attitudes toward the person, family, work, justice, commerce, worship, and human flourishing.

In their well-regarded book on economic development, *Why Nations Fail*, Daron Acemoglu and James Robinson make a distinction between what they call *inclusive* and *extractive* political and economic institutions.[1] Those countries that develop and succeed generally have inclusive institutions wherein many are included in the governing and, therefore, exploitation is diminished or absent. The nations that fail or remain poor have extractive institutions where the political class enjoys disproportional access to the nation's resources.

---

[*] Scripture quotations are taken from the Revised Standard Version (RSV).

[1] Daron Acemoglu and James Robinson, *Why Nations Fail: The Origins of Power, Prosperity, and Poverty* (New York: Crown Business, 2012).

There are many positive aspects to this book, which further develops Douglass North's theories of institutions,[2] but one serious weakness is that it radically detaches institutions from culture. I would argue that this is both a sociologically and a historically thin view of culture that does not do justice to the fact that institutions develop out of certain cultural conditions, assumptions, values, and beliefs. They cannot be separated from culture because they are also a product of culture.

The historian and sociologist Christopher Dawson has argued that the driving force of culture is not the economy or politics but, in fact, *cultus*—religion.[3] We cannot come to any serious understanding of a culture and the institutions that emerge from it if we do not take religion seriously. This is not to say we cannot live for a time under and benefit from institutions and economic arrangements without understanding their source, but cultural capital only lasts so long. If we are to understand the institutions that have brought about unparalleled wealth creation, it means we need to pay attention to the Jewish and Christian sources that produced them.

I am not suggesting that there are no important modern influences on these institutions or that certain Enlightenment figures did not provide positive contributions. As Lord Acton has demonstrated, the history of liberty is complex, and the development of these institutions was not a linear development.[4] There are a great number of modern influences—John Locke, Adam Smith, and Edmund Burke among others contributed a great deal—but none of their contributions were as important, nor could they have developed *except* for the influence of Judaism and Christianity. As the famous economic historian, Joseph Schumpeter, has written, there is very little in Adam Smith that did not already exist in the economic writings of medieval scholastic theologians.[5] These were thinkers heavily influenced by the philosophical works and biblical commentaries of St. Thomas Aquinas who, in turn, was influenced not only by the church fathers but also by

---

[2] See, for example, Douglass North, *Institutions, Institutional Change and Economic Performance* (New York: Cambridge University Press, 1990).

[3] See, *inter alia*, Christopher Dawson, *Religion and Culture* (London: Sheed & Ward, 1948).

[4] Lord Acton, "The History of Freedom in Christianity," in *Essays in the History of Liberty*, ed. J. R. Fears (Indianapolis: Liberty Classics, 1986).

[5] Joseph A. Schumpeter, *History of Economic Analysis* (New York: Oxford University Press, 1954).

medieval rabbinic commentators such as Maimonides and Rashi.[6] Simply put, these ideas did not pop out of nowhere.

The main focus of this chapter will be the Jewish and Christian sources of the institutions of private property. Before discussing property, though, I would like to briefly highlight various deeper cultural influences that come from Jewish and Christian traditions and that have profoundly impacted Western culture—from marriage and family, to politics, economics, and society—and that underlie the strong commitment to private property as a means to human flourishing.

View of the Human Person

A culture's understanding of the nature and destiny of the human person plays a key role in the development of politics and economics. As John Paul II argued, the primary fault of socialism was not economic or political, but anthropological.[7] The socialist economy and political system that had dominated his native Poland for decades found its roots in the materialist and reductionist view of the person. Socialist rejection of private property cannot be separated from its anthropology. In contrast, the biblical view of the person with its rich understanding of human freedom, moral agency, and a deep respect for reason had a tremendous impact on the development of the West—not only socially and morally but also economically and politically. The biblical view begins with man, created in the image of God.

> So God created man in his own image, in the image of God he created him; male and female he created them. And God blessed them, and God said to them, "Be fruitful and multiply, and fill the earth and subdue it; and have dominion over the fish of the sea and over the birds of the air and over every living thing that moves upon the earth." Gen. 1:27–28

The layers of meaning that derive from this simple passage—to be created in the image of God—are deep and rich; I could not possibly exhaust them in a lifetime of study, much less a short reflection. Nevertheless, we can say here that among other things this implies that man is distinct from the

---

[6] See, for example, Rabbi Herman Hailperin, *Rashi and the Christian Scholars* (Pittsburgh: University of Pittsburgh Press, 1963).

[7] John Paul II, Encyclical Letter *Centesimus Annus*, no. 13.

lower animals and that he is endowed with reason and free will. He is an embodied person who is to be seen and understood as a *subject*, an end in himself, and not simply an object to be used for another's gratification or to be organized simply for the good of the state. The biblical view of man is neither the radical individual of Hobbes or Rousseau nor a cog in a collectivist machine. The late Jesuit philosopher Norris Clarke explained this tension between individuality and community, describing the person as "substance-in-relationship."[8] Man is an individual person, a substance, but he is also a social being and he finds his fulfillment in relationship with others. He is born into a family; into language, culture, and so on, and these things shape him.

Finally, we see from the Genesis narrative, and later in the command to keep the Sabbath, that man is not simply a worker nor created for utility alone. He has an eternal destiny. To be sure, man was created to work, but he was also made for rest and for worship.[9]

This is of course a very brief and rough outline, but all of these ideas shape the way we understand society, work, physical matter, law, economics, and politics. When this view is lost or replaced, it has profound consequences.

This loss of the biblical concept of man has been most obvious in the area of human perfectibility, the idea that evil does not come from man himself but from society. Eric Voegelin argued that one of the dominant features of modern, secular politics is the idea of human perfectibility—the belief that evil can be eradicated in this world by human means through politics and economics.[10] If we can find the right way to organize the state, or education, or the economy, this way of thinking goes, then we can eliminate evil and create a perfectly just and equal society.

While Jews and Catholics have different understandings of the fall of Adam and Eve and the concept of original sin, both recognize that man's

---

[8] W. Norris Clarke, SJ, *Person and Being* (Milwaukee: Marquette University Press, 1993).

[9] In Genesis, God commands Adam to "till and keep" or to cultivate and guard the garden. The Hebrew words *avodah* and *shamar* also have a priestly connotation to them. *Avodah* means both work and worship. Furthermore, there is a repeating theme in both the Hebrew Bible and the books of the New Testament of man called to "enter into God's rest."

[10] Eric Voegelin, *The New Science of Politics: An Introduction* (1951; repr., Chicago: University of Chicago Press, 1987).

tendency to evil does not come from the outside and cannot be redeemed or perfected through politics.

Man is good, but he is fallen. Catholics and Jews do not believe that man is totally depraved but that there is something wrong, some disorder—what John Henry Newman called an "aboriginal calamity"—that cannot be fixed simply by rearranging the economic or social orders. This creates a resistance to utopian and totalitarian schemes and leads to a corollary: a deep hostility from totalitarian regimes to religion—especially Judaism.

Again, while each of these is more complex than this discussion reveals, the following are other examples of theological and religious influences on culture.

Time and Progress

The Jewish and Christian concept of time as linear, with a *telos*, has completely transformed the West. Even Nietzsche, who was no friend of Christians or Jews, admitted this.[11] The Jewish (and thereby Christian) idea of time and progress falls between the extremes of pagan cyclical fatalism and secular utopianism and the promise of heaven on earth.

Justice and Rule of Law

Western ideas of rule of law find their origins in the Hebrew Bible: Exodus 23:3; Exodus 6; and Leviticus 19:15 forbid partiality—either toward the rich or the poor. This is quite distinct from modern humanitarian or populist movements that believe that poverty or social status trumps justice.

Work

From the beginning of Genesis, we also see a deep respect for the value of work. Man is commanded to be fruitful and multiply, to cultivate the garden. It is important to note that work comes before the fall. Work itself is not a punishment or something to be escaped; it is a part of how man lives out his vocation and reflects the divine image.

Of course, work must be seen in the light of the Sabbath, which puts work and material gain in its proper place. Exodus 20:9–10 mandates this

---

[11] My co-panelist at the conference where I presented this paper, Zev Golan, suggested to me that while Nietzsche was indeed contemptuous of Christianity, his view of Judaism was more positive. Golan argues this case in *God, Man, and Nietzsche: A Startling Dialogue between Judaism and Modern Philosophers* (New York: iUniverse, 2007).

Sabbath rest: "Six days you shall labor, and do all your work; but the seventh day is a sabbath to the LORD your God." Man is made for more than work and leisure (understood as entertainment). Man is made for worship.[12]

It is also important to note that something unique regarding the treatment of work in the Hebrew Bible and the Jewish tradition is the affirmation not only of study and learning but also of manual labor, economic activity, and creation of value.

The Babylonian Talmud states: "A person should love work and not hate it; for just as the Torah was given with a covenant, so too was work given with a covenant." Furthermore, "If a person has no work to do, what should he do? If he has a dilapidated yard or field, he should go and occupy himself with it."[13]

This respect for manual labor continues in the Christian tradition. Saint Benedict writes in his famous rule that "Idleness is the enemy of the soul. Therefore, the monks should be occupied at certain times in manual labor, and at other fixed hours in holy reading."[14] The Benedictine motto of *ora et labora* is another affirmation of this positive view of work, including manual labor.

We see careful analysis of commercial life, buying, selling, and acquisition of property in Maimonides' Code Book 12 on the Code of Acquisitions (*Sefer Kinyan*) that amounts to three hundred pages in English.

The Hebrew Bible is very clear that all things ultimately belong to God, and we must be detached from wealth. It is important to note that there was no disdain for work or for commercial activity. Within the right order of things, they are viewed as positive.

Perhaps the best summary of the value and proper attitude toward commerce is found in the Wisdom literature, notably the Proverbs 31 description

---

[12] Some commentaries on the importance of Sabbath and the real meaning of leisure are Josef Pieper, *Leisure: The Basis of Culture*, trans. Alexander Dru (New York: Pantheon Books, 1958); Josef Pieper, *In Tune with the World: A Theory of Festivity*, trans. Richard and Clara Winston (New York: Harcourt, Brace, & World, 1965); Yosef Yitzhak Lifshitz, "Secret of the Sabbath," *Azure* 10 (Winter 2001): 85–117; Abraham Heschel, *The Sabbath: Its Meaning for Modern Man* (New York: Farrar, Straus, 1952); Pope John Paul II, Apostolic Letter *Dies Domini* (1998).

[13] Rabbi Yehuda ben Bathyra, Babylonian Talmud, Avot D'Rabbi Noson 11:1.

[14] Rule of St. Benedict, chapter 48, https://www.ewtn.com/library/PRIESTS/BENRULE.HTM.

of the valiant wife, who combines industry with wisdom and charity and becomes a blessing for others.

This positive view of commerce is very different from most other cultures where manual labor and work are seen as servile and beneath the dignity of the person. This was prevalent among the Greeks and even made its way into Christian Europe, which at times appropriated pagan/aristocratic disdain for commerce. This had a myriad of negative effects, preventing economic development and perpetuating poverty and creating hostility to productive segments of society—including, often, Jews.

Private Property

The preceding section merely touches on how the Jewish and Christian traditions have shaped culture; many other examples could be discussed. With this basic framework in place, however, I want to move on to a similar account of the role of private property in these religious traditions. First, I will briefly examine how this "institution of justice" finds its origins in Jewish and Christian traditions. Second, I will discuss some of the effects of private property on economics and society. This discussion will conclude with a brief analysis of the interconnection among private property, family, and religious liberty.

I want to be clear that I am in no way suggesting that the Bible advocates free-market capitalism or that serious Christians and Jews need to be supporters of a competitive economy. People of good will can disagree about a number of policy issues. What I am saying is that throughout Scripture and tradition we see an undeniable respect for private property, and this has an impact on how we understand economics.

The Jewish and Christian Roots of Private Property

Private property—both land and personal—has always been valued and protected within the Jewish and Christian traditions, and we see a concern for private property throughout the Hebrew Bible.

Theft and Restitution

Most evidently, we see private property presupposed in the Decalogue with the commandments in Exodus 20:15 and 20:17: "You shall not steal," and "You shall not covet your neighbor's house."

In Exodus 22, we find clear laws of how restitution must be made for stolen property, damaged property, dishonesty—even borrowed property that has been harmed. Exodus 22:1 and 4 states:

> If a man steals an ox or a sheep, and kills it or sells it, he shall pay five oxen for an ox, and four sheep for a sheep. He shall make restitution; if he has nothing, then he shall be sold for his theft. If the stolen beast is found alive in his possession, whether it is an ox or an ass or a sheep, he shall pay double.

Abuse of Private Property, Injustice, Defrauding, Exploitation

These are condemned throughout the Bible—most emphatically in the Prophets such as Amos, Ezekiel, and Isaiah. Isaiah 3:14–15 proclaims:

> The LORD enters into judgment with the elders and princes of his people: "It is you who have devoured the vineyard, the spoil of the poor is in your houses. What do you mean by crushing my people, by grinding the face of the poor?" says the Lord GOD of hosts.

Land and Family

On a deeper level, we see private property, specifically land, regarded both for its economic value and for its connection to family, worship, and social cohesion. Property and land are major themes in God's covenant with Abraham in Genesis 13 when God promises the land to Abraham.

There is an interesting passage in Genesis 23 that specifically relates to the issue of land titling—which is a serious problem throughout the developing world as I will discuss later.

In Genesis 23, Abraham is trying to buy a burial plot for his wife Sarah. The Hittites are willing to give it to him, but Abraham says no, he wants to pay for it: "For the full price let him give it to me in your presence as a possession for a burying place" (v. 9). He pays the four hundred shekels of silver and the land is "made over to Abraham as a possession in the presence of the Hittites" (vv. 17–18).

Charity

We also see that charity, religious duty, and sacrifice presuppose private property. For example, the people are obliged to offer sacrifice and first fruits to God (Ex. 23:19; 34:26); to tithe (Lev. 27:30; Deut. 14:22); and to be generous with the poor (Deut. 15:11).

The idea that sacrifice must be done from one's own possessions is also seen in 2 Samuel 24. David wants to build an altar at the threshing floor of Ara-unah the Jubusite who offers David his property and cattle, but David declines and insists that he needs to buy it: "I will not offer burnt offerings to the LORD my God which cost me nothing" (v. 24).

Private Property and Stewardship

Property is connected to stewardship and ultimately all property belongs to God. Consider Deuteronomy 8:17–18: "Beware lest you say in your heart, 'My power and the might of my hand have gotten me this wealth.' ... for it is [the Lord] who gives you power to get wealth." There are many other examples of the respect for private property. In 1 Samuel 8 and 12 one of the marks of just leadership is to respect property and to not defraud the people. When the people ask for a king, Samuel says: "Testify against me before the LORD.... Whose ox have I taken?" (12:3).

In 1 Kings 21, we see how Jezebel and Ahab are punished severely for abusing power and for stealing Naboth's Vineyard. Here, too, we see the connection between private property and the family; Naboth does not want to sell his family inheritance.

New Testament

The New Testament continues the Hebrew Bible's view of property and stewardship. In the Gospels, Jesus commands the people not to steal, not to covet, to share, to give their things to the poor, and not to be attached to riches. In Ephesians 4:28, Paul says, "Let the thief no longer steal, but rather let him labor, doing honest work with his hands, so that he may be able to give to those in need."

There is, however, one episode in the New Testament that has generated some confusion about the Christian view of private property. Acts 4 and 5 speak of a community in Jerusalem where all the believers were of one heart and mind and no one claimed anything as his own but held everything in common. Ananias and Sapphira sell their property and give the proceeds to this community but secretly hold some of it back. Their lie is discovered and they are both struck dead. Some have questioned whether this passage is evidence that early Christianity rejected private property and advocated communal ownership as the ideal. Yet if we look at it more closely, we can see that this is not the case.

In fact, Peter does not deny private property, but reaffirms it. He says in Acts 5:4:

> While it remained unsold, did it not remain your own? And after it was sold, was it not at your disposal? How is it that you have contrived this deed in your heart? You have not lied to men but to God.

What we see from these passages is neither the denial of private property nor a radical departure from Judaism. First, while people are indeed giving up private property, it is voluntary and not required. Second, the punishment was for lying to God, not for keeping private property. Third, this was an early model of monasticism, which continues today and, again, is voluntary. Finally, it is important to remember that in the cases of the community in Acts and also in ancient and contemporary monasticism, the property is still *private*. It is not owned by the state.

While Christian monasticism may be a departure from Judaism, the idea that the New Testament somehow favors a type of public ownership of property is untenable. What we see instead is the affirmation and continuation of respect for private property within the framework of stewardship and justice. This position has been affirmed and repeated throughout the centuries. The Church's preeminent medieval theologian, St. Thomas Aquinas, deals directly with the issue of private property in question 66 of the *Summa Theologica*. In article 1, Aquinas affirms private property as stemming from man's dominion over the earth and his capacity to reason because he is created in the divine image. He also rejects those who argue that Scripture calls for renouncing private property. In article 2, he argues that it is lawful and necessary for men to have private property,

> First, because every man is more careful to procure what is for himself alone than that which is common to many or to all.
>
> Secondly, because human affairs are conducted in more orderly fashion if each man is charged with taking care of something particular...
>
> Thirdly, because a more peaceful state is ensured to man if each one is contented with his own—and quarrels arise more frequently where there is no division of the things possessed.[15]

---

[15] Thomas Aquinas, *Summa Theologica*, II–II, q. 66, art. 2.

In modern Catholic social teaching from Leo XIII's *Rerum Novarum* to the present, private property has been consistently reaffirmed as well.

The Effects of Private Property

Having established the essential support for private property with Judaism and Christianity, we turn to the question of the practical effects of the ownership of property. Why is private property important and what happens when you do not have it?

Enables Economic Development

First, private property is a *sine qua non* for economic development and economic inclusion. In many countries throughout the world, 50 to 60 percent of the land has no clear title. If you do not know who owns the land, then you have no incentive to improve and develop it, and it can be easily taken away from you—especially if you are a widow or an orphan.

Without clear title, you also cannot use the land as collateral to get a loan. As Peruvian economist Hernando De Soto points out, the existing assets in the developing world are much greater than all the foreign aid over the last decades; the problem is that the poor cannot access the value of their land without clear title. What results is much potentially productive land that remains unproductive.[16]

Consider the contrast to Israel in the late 1800s when much of the land that is now highly productive and fertile was arid or malarial swamps. Private property and title can have tremendous effects on economic productivity. If we overlay maps of economic development and property rights, we see strong correlation between the two.

Changes Worldview

The second thing private property does is change the way you see the world. Rafael Di Tella and Ernesto Schargrosky conducted an interesting study in a neighborhood in Buenos Aires where half of the people got title to their land, and the other half was still waiting to get title. They discovered that having clear title to land actually changed the way in which people saw the world. Those with clear title to their land had higher levels of trust, lower rates of teenage pregnancy, more concern for education, and a more positive

---

[16] Hernando de Soto, *The Mystery of Capital: Why Capitalism Triumphs in the West and Fails Everywhere Else* (New York: Basic Books, 2000).

outlook toward the future. While many of their preferences in music and entertainment remained the same as their neighbors, their attitude toward the future and society became similar to that of middle-class Argentineans.[17]

Limits the State

The third thing private property does is limit the state. It does so in at least a couple of ways. Most obviously, when property is not owned by the state but by different private interests, this creates different centers of power and influence and creates resistance to state power. Private property not only enables private businesses to flourish but also enables stronger layers of civil society or what Alexis de Tocqueville called "intermediary institutions." These include schools, private associations, synagogues, churches, mutual aid societies, and the like, which create a buffer between the individual and the state. Along with the family, all of these things are essential in preventing deracination and resisting radical individualism.

One of the great insights of Tocqueville is that individualism leads to centralization. When families, religious communities, and civil society are weak or nonexistent, there are few layers between the individual and the state, and the state begins to absorb more things to itself—ultimately leading to what he called "soft despotism."[18] Tocqueville writes that what prevents this descent into soft despotism are three things: local politics, civil society (private voluntary organizations), and religion.

Each of these pulls people out of themselves and gets them engaged in their communities and with others. Yet, without private property, people are not as involved in their community and can easily became wards and pawns of the state. This is another reason why schools and religious communities need to be careful about what kind of support they receive from the state: this can easily be used to co-opt them for the state's purposes.

Promotes Family and Religious Liberty

Finally, private property is essential for the family and, by the same token, for religious liberty. Property creates the space for families to live out their freedoms and responsibilities. It enables families to have economic independence and not simply be dependent on others. This space and

---

[17] Rafael Di Tella, Sebastian Galiani, and Ernesto Schargrodsky, "The Formation of Beliefs: Evidence from the Allocation of Land Titles to Squatters," *Quarterly Journal of Economics* 122 (February 2007): 209–41.

[18] Alexis de Tocqueville, *Democracy in America*, 2, bk. 4, chap. 6.

independence is essential for the religion and culture, for where is religion and culture primarily passed down? Not first and foremost in the church, synagogue, or religious school—but in the family. Without the freedom of the family, there cannot long be freedom of religion.

While Catholics and Jews can at times forget the interconnection among family, property, and religion, socialists have understood it well. Socialists of almost every stripe from Marx and Engels, to Robert Owen, Gramsci, the Fabians, and the Frankfurt School all recognize the reinforcing nature of these three things—this is why they always fight to eradicate them. Friedrich Engels, quoting Robert Owen, maintained that there were three primary obstacles to socialist reform: "private property, religion, the present form of marriage."[19]

As Jewish and Christian teaching and socialist writers recognize, there is a deep and reinforcing relationship between private property and religion, and when private property rights are harmed, families are weakened, religious liberty is endangered, and the door to soft and hard despotic states is opened.

Conclusion

We can often reduce economics to questions of utility or productivity or focus on policy issues. While private property is indeed an economic issue, its effects go far beyond economics. Private property not only creates economic value, it promotes human flourishing, protects the poor, and creates the space for religious practice and for families to live out their freedom and responsibilities.

This is also a much stronger rhetorical position in the face of impassioned religious or humanitarian arguments against property and the market as forces of exploitation. At a time when there is increasing suspicion toward free economies and private property, both on secular and religious fronts, it is important for those who value it to make not only the economic or efficiency case for private property but, more importantly, to show how it benefits the poor, promotes human flourishing, and protects religious liberty—ultimately because it respects the dignity of the human person, made for freedom, made for family, and endowed with intelligence to solve problems and steward God's creation.

---

[19] Frederick Engels, *Socialism: Utopian and Scientific* (1880), https://www.marxists.org/archive/marx/works/1880/soc-utop/ch01.htm.

Appendix

Remarks on the Concept of Religious Liberty[*]

Michael Novak

It is a joy to be working once again with the Acton Institute. I think it may be fair to say, at least metaphorically, that the initial idea for the Institute was born around Karen's and my dining room table on Northampton Street in Washington, DC, while Father Sirico was still a seminarian with the Paulist Fathers. Often when we had one of Karen's famous dinners, she would ask Father Sirico to make one of his amazingly good *antipasti*. (Clare Boothe Luce asked him for his recipe.)

Tonight, in brief, even telegraphic form, I would like to lay out the argument of the American Founding Fathers on religious liberty—notably Thomas Jefferson and James Madison (with George Mason in the background)—which they regarded as the foundation of all natural rights. In the context of world history, their argument marks one of the chief points of originality that the Americans brought to the tradition of natural rights.

Like the Second Vatican Council's *Dignitatis Humanae*, the American Founders began their exposition of the meaning of rights with a concept of *duty*—and along with that, the concept of an *inalienable* duty. Here is how they proceeded.

---

[*] These remarks were delivered during a reception at the Acton Institute's event, Acton University in Grand Rapids, Michigan, June 16, 2015.

The first building block of their argument was the concept of duty, a primordial and self-evident duty, evident to anyone who grasped the full meaning of the concepts of *Creator* and *creature*. It was self-evident to the founders that:

1. the creature owed her entire existence to the insight and will of the Creator. Without the Creator, the creature would have no ability even to be conscious or to perform deliberate actions. Thus, any conscious creature who did not show profound gratitude to his Creator would rightly be self-condemned as an ingrate.
2. the creature who grasps the total, transcendent disparity between Creator and creature would recognize, with equal self-evidence, his duty not only to pay gratitude but also to worship the Creator. For the power and intelligence of the Creator would so far surpass the creature's that adoration would be the only fitting response.
3. while the Creator could have forced creatures to recognize these duties of gratitude and worship, "the Divine Author" of the religion of the Founders (the Christian religion), expressly created humans *free* and decreed that "free they shall remain."

Thus, while self-evidently all creatures owe their Creator the twin duties of gratitude and worship, the founders argued, each human being had a right *and an obligation* to exercise these duties as his or her free conscience directed.

For this account of their reasoning on the right of liberty of conscience, the main references are:

1. George Mason's wording of paragraph sixteen of the Virginia Declaration of Rights:

   That religion, or the duty which we owe to our Creator, and the manner of discharging it, can be directed only by reason and conviction, not by force or violence; and therefore all men are equally entitled to the free exercise of religion, according to the dictates of conscience; and that it is the mutual duty of all to practice Christian forbearance, love, and charity toward each other;

2. Thomas Jefferson's Virginia Statute for Religious Freedom;

3. James Madison's *Memorial and Remonstrance* against Governor Patrick Henry's proposal to tax all religious believers to support religious education in the schools (in almost all of which the teachers were Anglican ministers who, now disestablished, were no longer receiving salaries from the state). In his *Remonstrance*, Madison spelled out more clearly than anyone before him the reasons for using the term *inalienable duties*. First, these duties came directly from God and thus could not be taken away or restricted by anyone short of the Creator—not by one's own family or friends or the state or even civil society. Further, these duties were inalienable also with respect to the individual human being, for the Creator imposed them directly on every creature capable of reflection and choice. These duties inhere in the human person and in no one else.

The founders went on to make another distinction. Although the concepts and the logic that underlie their declaration of religious liberty flow from a Jewish and Christian concept of reality, in order to put them into practice, no one needed to confess Christian faith. The original articulation of the principles underlying the declaration lay clearly in sources that are Jewish and Christian in inspiration. Other conscious creatures of the Creator also subject to these universal duties did not need to profess Jewish or Christian faith in order to practice them. The words *inalienable duty* may have had a Christian origin, but the duty did not.

In this sense, the declarations of Mason, Jefferson, and Madison, were self-abnegating. There is a difference between the *genesis* of the first articulation of religious liberties and the *practice* of these principles in a manner rooted in other cultures and other lines of argument. Their practice in other cultures and traditions could spring from other reasons and motives. For instance, religious freedom may be practiced for reasons of public peace, good order, and social amity, or it may be inspired by the teachings of other religions.

To summarize, we begin with the *duty* that all creatures owe to their Creator, and with the further duty imposed on each human person exercising these duties to the Creator in the light of personal conscience. We might even say, "in the light of cultural conscience rooted in other cultures and traditions."

I have also outlined the origins and reasons for the concepts of *self-evidence*, *inalienable duties*, and *natural rights*. Finally, I underline the potential cultural pluralism of justifications for the principles of religious liberty.

Over the next few days, you will have the chance to begin figuring out what your own intellect and conscience teach you, as an individual person, about your duties and rights regarding religious liberty. That is the point of this university: to help each of us think for ourselves, and appropriate—that is, make our own, assimilate into our own minds and hearts in our own personal way—the key lessons of the tradition of religious liberty as history has brought it down to us. The intellectual work of establishing religious liberty has not yet been completed. Far from it! Most of the peoples of the world, even today, do not enjoy such liberty. The opponents of religious liberty are many and are active. Steps forward in this tradition are often battered backward. Fulfilling the duty is often a battle.

About the Authors

ZEV GOLAN is senior research fellow at the Jerusalem Institute for Market Studies. Golan was director of Israel's Institute for Advanced Strategic and Political Studies from 1992 to 2003. His economic commentary has appeared in *Globes*, *Haaretz*, and the *Jerusalem Post*. He has edited over a hundred studies of the Israeli economy. Golan's historical research focuses on the Jewish people's struggle for freedom. His books include *Stern: The Man and His Gang*; *Free Jerusalem*; *God, Man and Nietzsche*; and *An Economy in Crisis* (Hebrew). His play, *The Ghosts of Mizrachi Bet Street*, based on the life of underground leader Abraham Stern, was performed at the Jerusalem Theater in 2016.

SAMUEL GREGG is director of research at the Acton Institute. He has written and spoken extensively on political economy, economic history, ethics in finance, and natural law theory. He has a master of arts in political philosophy from the University of Melbourne, and a doctor of philosophy degree in moral philosophy and political economy from the University of Oxford. He is the author of many books, including *On Ordered Liberty* (2003), *The Modern Papacy* (2009), *Becoming Europe: Economic Decline, Culture, and How America Can Avoid a European Future* (2013), and *For God and Profit: How Banking and Finance Can Serve the Common Good* (2016). His articles have appeared in journals such as the *Harvard Journal of Law and Public Policy*; *Journal of Markets & Morality*; *Economic Affairs*; *Journal des Economistes et des Etudes Humaines*; *Notre Dame Journal of Law, Ethics and Public Policy*; *Oxford Analytica*; *Communio*; *Foreign*

Affairs; and *Policy*. His opinion pieces have appeared in the *Wall Street Journal Europe*; *National Review*; *Public Discourse*; *American Spectator*; *Australian Financial Review*; and *Business Review Weekly*. He has been elected to the Royal Historical Society (2001), the Mont Pèlerin Society (2004), the Philadelphia Society (2008) and the Royal Economic Society (2008).

SANTIAGO LEGARRE is professor of law at Pontificia Universidad Católica Argentina and also works at CONICET (Argentine National Council for the Research in the Humanities). In addition, he is a visiting professor at the Notre Dame Law School, the Paul M. Hebert Law Center, Louisiana State University, and the Valparaiso University Law School (Indiana). He has been a visiting scholar at Columbia University, the University of Oxford, and the University of Notre Dame. Legarre studied for his bachelor of laws at the Universidad Católica Argentina, and for his master of studies in legal research at the University of Oxford. He also holds a doctorate in law from the Universidad de Buenos Aires. He has authored and contributed to a number of books and has published numerous articles on morality, law, history, and politics.

ARCHBISHOP MAROUN LAHHAM is auxiliary bishop and vicar of the Latin Patriarch of Jerusalem for Jordan. A native of Jordan, Archbishop Lahham has written and translated many books and articles on adult catechesis, Christian spirituality, peace in the Holy Land, the significance of Jerusalem, interreligious dialogue, Christian anthropology, and the history of the Latin Patriarchate. In 1972, he was ordained a priest in Jerusalem, having completed his philosophical and theological studies at the Latin Patriarchate Seminary in Beit Jala, where he received a bachelor's degree in philosophy and theology. He studied in Rome from 1988 to 1992, earning a doctorate in pastoral theology and catechesis at the Pontifical Lateran University. He has served as director general of the Latin Patriarchate Schools, rector of the Patriarchal Seminary in Beit Jala, and Bishop of Tunis. In 2010, Pope Benedict XVI raised Tunis to an Archdiocese and Bishop Lahham was appointed its first archbishop. He was recalled to the Middle East and appointed to his current position in 2012.

DANIEL MARK is assistant professor of political science at Villanova University, where he is also a faculty associate of the Matthew J. Ryan Center for the Study of Free Institutions and the Public Good. He serves on the US Commission on International Religious Freedom and has participated in USCIRF delegations to Azerbaijan, Indonesia, Malaysia, Nigeria, and Vietnam. He has written on international religious freedom for *Foreign Affairs*, *US News & World Report*, *Investor's Business Daily*, and the *Philadelphia Inquirer*. He has been interviewed on CNN, Al Jazeera America, and CBS radio in Philadelphia. He is an assistant editor of *Interpretation: A Journal of Political Philosophy*, a fellow of the Witherspoon Institute, and a contributor to *Arc of the Universe: Ethics and Global Justice*. He has also taught at the Straus Center for Torah and Western Thought at Yeshiva University. He holds bachelor's, master's, and doctoral degrees from the Department of Politics at Princeton University where his supervisor was Professor Robert P. George. For the 2015–2016 academic year, he was a visiting fellow in the Department of Politics at Princeton University under the sponsorship of the James Madison Program in American Ideals and Institutions.

MICHAEL MATHESON MILLER is research fellow and director of Acton Media at the Acton Institute. He lectures internationally on moral philosophy, economic development, and entrepreneurship. He is a frequent guest on radio and has been published in the *Washington Times*, *Detroit News*, *LA Daily News*, and *Real Clear Politics*. He is the director and host of the PovertyCure DVD Series and has appeared in various video curricula including *Doing the Right Thing*, *Effective Stewardship*, and *The Birth of Freedom*. Before coming to Acton, he taught philosophy and political science and was the chair of the philosophy and theology department at Ave Maria College of the Americas in Nicaragua. Miller received a bachelor's degree from the University of Notre Dame, a master's from Nagoya University's Graduate School of International Development (Japan), a master's in philosophy from Franciscan University, and a master of business administration in international management from Thunderbird Graduate School of Global Business. He serves on the President's Advisory Council of Aquinas College in Nashville, the board of the Dietrich von Hildebrand Legacy Project, and the board of trustees for Angelico Press.

MICHAEL NOVAK is visiting professor and trustee at Ave Maria University in Florida. A theologian, author, and former US ambassador, he held the George Frederick Jewett Chair in Religion, Philosophy, and Public Policy at the American Enterprise Institute in Washington, DC. For his work and influence, he has received many international awards, including the 1994

Templeton Prize for Progress in Religion. Novak has written numerous influential books on economics, philosophy, and theology. His masterpiece, *The Spirit of Democratic Capitalism*, was published underground in Poland in 1984, and after 1989 in Czechoslovakia, Germany, China, Hungary, Bangladesh, Korea, and many times in Latin America.

ANIELKA (MÜNKEL) OLSON is an adjunct professor at Spring Arbor University. She was previously project manager at the Acton Institute, where she was co-producer of the Poverty, Inc. documentary and the PovertyCure DVD Series. A native and citizen of Nicaragua, she served as advisor to Nicaragua's minister of tourism. She collaborated on speeches for former President Enrique Bolaños and negotiated investment opportunities with international corporations. Previously, she served as coordinator of the Government Investor Network (GIN) at PRONicaragua, the Investment Promotion Agency of the Presidency. She also authored "Nicaragua: A UN Pilot Country on the Road to Success" and was selected to participate in the US Department of State International Visitor Leadership Program. Olson holds a master of business administration from the University of Notre Dame, where she won the grand prize in the Social Venture Plan Competition with Sustainable Health Enterprises.

FATHER MARTIN RHONHEIMER is professor of ethics and philosophy at the Pontifical University of the Holy Cross in Rome. A native of Zurich, Switzerland, Fr. Rhonheimer studied philosophy, history, political science, and theology in Zurich and Rome. He joined the personal prelature Opus Dei in 1974 and was ordained a priest in 1983. His main interests lie in the fields of ethics, action theory, and the history of classical liberalism and economics. He has published on a wide range of topics, especially concerning the philosophy of moral action, virtue, natural law, Aquinas, and Aristotle; the ethics of sexuality and bioethics; and, more recently, on philosophical and ethical questions concerning the economic order.

JAY W. RICHARDS is assistant research professor in the School of Business and Economics at the Catholic University of America, a senior fellow at the Discovery Institute, and executive editor of *The Stream*. He has authored and co-authored many books, including the *New York Times* bestsellers *Infiltrated* and *Indivisible*. He is also executive producer of several television documentaries, including *The Call of the Entrepreneur* and *The Birth of Freedom*.

Richards's articles and essays have been published in the *Harvard Business Review*, *Washington Post*, *Wall Street Journal*, *Investor's Business Daily*, *Forbes*, *National Review*, *Washington Times*, *Philadelphia Inquirer*, *Huffington Post*, *American Spectator*, and many other publications. He has appeared on hundreds of radio and television programs and has lectured at dozens of college and university campuses in the United States, Europe, and Asia; at many think tanks in the United States and Europe; and, on several occasions, to members of the US Congress and their staffs. Richards holds a doctorate in philosophy and theology from Princeton Theological Seminary, a master's of divinity, a master's of theology, and a bachelor of arts in political science and religion.

CARDINAL ROBERT SARAH is the prefect of the Congregation for Divine Worship and the Discipline of the Sacraments. He was born in Ourous in the Archdiocese of Conakry in Guinea and was ordained a priest in 1969. He obtained a licentiate in theology from the Pontifical Gregorian University in Rome and also studied at the Pontifical Biblical Institute there. In addition, he holds a licentiate in Sacred Scriptures from the Studium Biblicum Franciscanum in Jerusalem. In Guinea, he has served as a parish priest and rector of the junior seminary of Kindia. He was appointed archbishop of Conakry in 1979 where he served until 2001 when he was appointed secretary of the Congregation for the Evangelization of Peoples. In 2010, Pope Benedict XVI appointed him president of the "Cor Unum" Pontifical Council, the dicastery charged with coordinating the charitable activities of the Church. He was also elevated to the College of Cardinals. Pope Francis named him prefect of the Congregation for Divine Worship in 2014.

KEVIN SCHMIESING is research fellow at the Acton Institute where he edits the Christian Social Thought Series. A graduate of Franciscan University of Steubenville, he also holds a doctorate in American history from the University of Pennsylvania. He is the author of dozens of books, articles, and book reviews in the fields of religious history, Catholic social teaching, and the history of economics, which have appeared in the *Journal of Church and State*, *University of St. Thomas Law Journal*, *Catholic Social Science Review*, *Logos*, *Catholic Historical Review*, *Journal of American History*, and many other print and online outlets. Schmiesing serves as second vice president of the Society of Catholic Social Scientists. He teaches Church history in the Lay Pastoral Ministry Program of the Archdiocese of Cincinnati, and is a regular guest on the SonRise Morning Show, part of the EWTN Global Catholic Radio Network.

About the Authors

CARDINAL JOSEPH ZEN ZE-KIUN is bishop emeritus of Hong Kong. He was born in 1932 in Yang King-pang, Shanghai, China, and ordained a priest in 1961 for the Society of Don Bosco (Salesians). Cardinal Zen served as a Salesian provincial superior for China for six years. After completing his doctorate in Rome, he taught in seminaries in Hong Kong, mainland China, and Macao. In 1996, he was appointed coadjutor of the Diocese of Hong Kong, and, in 2002, was made bishop of the diocese. In this capacity, he emerged as a leading advocate of religious freedom in China. He was proclaimed cardinal by Pope Benedict XVI in the consistory of March 2006.